Overcoming the Seven Deadly Emotions

MICHELLE BORQUEZ

author of GOD CRAZY

HARVEST HOUSE PUBLISHERS

EUGENE, OREGON

Cover by Koechel Peterson & Associates, Inc., Minneapolis, Minnesota

OVERCOMING THE SEVEN DEADLY EMOTIONS
Copyright © 2008 by Michelle Borquez
Published by Harvest House Publishers
Eugene, Oregon 97402
www.harvesthousepublishers.com

Library of Congress Cataloging-in-Publication Data
Borquez, Michelle.
Overcoming the seven deadly emotions / Michelle Borquez.
    p. cm.
Includes bibliographical references.
ISBN-13: 978-0-7369-2139-8 (pbk.)
ISBN-10: 0-7369-2139-7 (pbk.)
1. Emotions—Religious aspects—Christianity. 2. Deadly sins. I. Title.
BV4597.3.B67 2008
248.4—dc22
                                                      2008002968

To my Lord and Savior—Lord, without You I am nothing. It is in You I have found my freedom, my joy again. I want to live in the eternal. Help me to hear You, to see You, and to never believe the lies but embrace the truth of who You are. You are everything in this life. Nothing satisfies but You…nothing.

To my dad, Pastor Tony Hormillosa—Dad, I am so thankful to know you. As I write these words my eyes well up with tears. I am overjoyed that after so many years of not really knowing you or feeling close to you, I am given the honor of seeing into your heart. I found my healing prior, but what a true blessing to have sealed it with your love and your admiration of me. Who knew?…God knew. His mercies are new every morning. I am so proud to be your daughter and to have gleaned from your determining commitment to Jesus Christ and ministry.

MICHELLE

To my children, Joshua, Aaron, Madison, and Jacob—Thank you for your continued support of the work of Christ in my life. I pray each one of you lives in the emotional and spiritual freedom Christ has for you. Nothing I do can be more of an accomplishment than imparting truth into your lives…so you also can impart truth to others. You are precious to me.

MOMMY

And to you who live in a place of quiet desperation—God sees. Your freedom is as close to you as the air surrounding you. Embrace the emotional and spiritual freedom awaiting you. Through Christ you shall find your victory.

Acknowledgments

*A wise man is full of strength, and a man of knowledge
enhances his might, for by wise guidance you can wage your
war, and in abundance of counselors there is victory.*

PROVERBS 24:5-6

I could not have embraced emotional and spiritual healing without a multitude of counselors. It all goes back to the very first counselors in my life, my mom and dad, Tony and Sandy Hormillosa. Thank you for imparting wisdom and guidance in my life. It's a beautiful privilege to be in a big family and see Christ glorified through the action of loving beyond failure and frailty. I am also deeply grateful to counselor Wes Harbour for tremendous support, Ruth Ann Johnson for godly mentoring, Dr. Catherine Hart Weber for advice and friendship, and finally to counselor Dale Dunnewold—thank you for pointing me to the truth of Christ when I couldn't see it and for exposing lies so that I could finally be free. I'm a new person...a free person...a victorious person.

Thanks to Bill Anderson Jr. Dear friend, thank you for your wisdom on "The Power to Be Free." You are a strong tower and a great man of God.

Thank you to Josh McDermott for your commitment to God Crazy Ministries. You are a dear brother in Christ.

Many thanks to Carolyn McCready of Harvest House, for your friendship and continued belief in me. Hope Lyda, you're amazing. Thank you for partnering with me on this book. Terry Glaspey and LaRae Weikert, thanks for friendship and great input. To the rest of the Harvest House gang, thanks for the amazing job you do.

To my God Crazy team of women who are just as radical as they come. You girls make me laugh, cry, and have fun. Thank you for loving me.

Contents

Foreword

Catherine Hart Weber

O ne of my favorite verses is Philippians 4:6-9, probably because I've had to learn how to apply it in my life and help others do the same—over and over again. Here is my paraphrase.

> Don't get all stressed out, concerned, fearful, nervous, worried, or overwhelmed by negative emotion and any of the challenges of life. Instead, calm down and tell God all about everything earnestly in prayer. Fully transfer the burdens of your soul into God's hands. Invite Him into the situations in your life, to change and heal the pain in your heart. When you entrust all your cares to Christ instead of fretting over them, you will experience emotional freedom and the peace of God in your mind and emotions instead of nagging anxiety. Then you can listen to His Spirit for guidance as He leads you into healthier actions. Our emotions, character, and actions begin in the way we think. So concentrate on things that are uplifting and positive, which will result in right living. Then you will have God's peace.

Don't you long for this calmness of mind, tranquility, and peace in your soul? Wouldn't it be great to "master" the storms of destructive emotion that seem to derail you and steal your joy, peace, and happiness? Well, God says there is a way. It is possible, even if you have an emotional, passionate temperament. Michelle will lead you in this better way as she candidly shares about her journey to emotional freedom. She will inspire you when you are overpowered by negative emotion and saying, "I just can't help it." Although it is challenging, you can learn both how and why to "help it" and discover that with the help of God's powerful love and the Holy Spirit, "you can."

God has created us with emotions, and they are an essential part of our lives. But understanding and dealing with the emotions representing deep pain and confusion that have a big impact on our lives can get complicated. My father, Dr. Archibald Hart, in his book *Unlocking the Mystery of Your Emotions,* starts out by saying that "the greatest battle the self must wage is against the emotions. The surest sign of maturity is the ability to experience one's emotions freely and integrate them into all aspects of one's being." Michelle will walk alongside you on this journey to maturity and emotional freedom, showing how you can learn to control and purify your thoughts and keep your emotions from overruling your soul and destroying your peace and potential.

I was standing in a long line at a busy cell phone store recently when a man at the counter got so frustrated with the worker that he slammed his cell phone down on the ground and started screaming and swearing. It only took a few long seconds for him to come to his senses in embarrassment, realizing he had lost control. Everyone in the store was in shock, but on a deeper level, I think we could all relate. But for the grace of God, at any time we could all be at risk of being overtaken by our emotions and a stress response.

We are truly wonderfully made, including all our emotions that are regulated in the limbic system of our brain (known as the "emotional brain" or the "heart"). Our deepest, primary emotions of love, joy, hope, desire, anger, hate, fear, surprise, and sadness originate from this center of our brain. It is in this place that we invite God to change and heal. This is also the center for our stress response, where our emotions are triggered and processed. The emotional brain alerts the body by sending out hormonal signals to react and respond. Depending on the brain's recommended response, some hormones are sent to calm the body down and some to bring a sense of love and desire. The stress response will signal for the body to either run or freeze up. In the phone store, the man's brain response signaled stress hormones of energy to fight back. Although his deep primary emotion could have been fear, his behavior reflected a secondary emotion of anger.

Thankfully God has created us with the capacity to evaluate events, weigh options, and control our emotions in what is considered the "thinking brain." However, when the emotional brain takes over the thinking brain, "flooding" happens that hijacks the brain so it reacts in ways we often regret. Sound familiar? We all experience this in big and small ways.

As Michelle shows us, if not controlled, these destructive emotions can sour our lives and ruin all that is sweet and beautiful. Our lack of self-control over our emotions can destroy our poise of character, our happiness, our health, our well-being, and our relationships. Even more sobering, we can stay in negative patterns that keep us from the abundant life God desires for us.

If you struggle to get a grip on your emotions, you don't have to battle it alone. Michelle will show you how you can control and purify your thoughts and keep your emotions from overruling your soul. As you read her engaging, transparent journey to emotional freedom, may you also find strength by using the power of God's Word, learning to choose the way of the Spirit, having self-control to calm the raging storms in your heart, and finding healing that only the peace of God can give.

Grace and peace to you,

Catherine Hart Weber, Ph.D.,
psychotherapist, adjunct professor at
Fuller Theological Seminary, author of
A Woman's Guide to Overcoming Depression

From Victim to Victor

Everything we do is either an act of love or a cry for help.

MARIANNE WILLIAMSON

I'm only half-joking when I say I was born with "too emotional" syndrome. As a young person I hated how easily affected I was by situations, comments, responses, or judgments. I remember dreading our yearly family get-together with all the cousins, aunts, uncles, and grandparents. Such family celebrations should be a time of joyful anticipation. However, in the days leading up to this gathering, I'd anticipate it with anxiety. By the time the day of the family event arrived, my nerves were on edge. It didn't take long before I was responding with heightened emotions to any negative word, sideways glance, or gesture that I interpreted as rejection.

Certainly my family was not out to get me. But this event, with all of the activity, noise, personalities, and opinions, was the perfect setting for my emotions to go haywire. I lost perspective. I lost the ability to filter input from the outside world (my family) and to filter the output (my surging emotions, including fear, shame, and anger). I was raw. A single criticism or even constructive comment from one of my cousins would send me spinning into an emotional state of despair...or at least a round of "woe is me" rejection. A lot of my response was based on the tremendous insecurities I had as a child, but it was also based on the overwhelming fear I had of people and their view of me.

Even at home, where I was most comfortable, my brothers and sister would tease me about my sensitivity. For much of my life I saw my sensitive, emotional nature as a weakness. I'm telling you, it's a sad day when you are getting emotional about being emotional! Clearly, something had to shift in my life.

What I have found as I have walked out my Christian journey is that God continues to refine my character so He is able to use my gifting and I am free to walk in my purpose. Part of this journey of refinement has been in the area of learning: learning to control my emotions so they don't control me and learning to respond to people, situations, and the rise of any emotion in a way that is glorifying to God. It has been a journey indeed. Truth be told, this part of my faith walk has resembled more of a climb at some points in my life. I've had to lean on God and work toward stronger, more godly emotional well-being.

If God didn't temper my personality, I might easily take on the burdens of the world—but guess what, that is not my job (nor is that your job). Praise God—someone already did that. We are not responsible to rescue anyone or save them, just to point them to the One who can save them, who can rescue them—Jesus.

This book isn't for those who are in a state of severe depression. I would never want anyone facing serious issues with anger or anxiety to bypass godly counsel. This book is not even a self-help book, a "positive thinking" book, or a book on psychotherapy. *Overcoming the Seven Deadly Emotions* is focused on spiritual growth in an area that is often ignored or glossed over as we pursue training in disciplines that seem more important, such as Scripture study, prayer, fellowship, and ministry. We'll examine the ways we conceal our deadly emotions from ourselves and others and how we master the art of sidestepping responsibility to understand and control our emotions and their influence, role, and potential (for good or bad) in our lives. Absolute clarity and truth are required for us to move from victim to victor in this significant area of our spiritual, emotional, and, I would even say, physical well-being. Our lifestyles are intertwined with our emotional approach to life. As we move toward exposing and overcoming the deadly emotions in our lives, we move toward the emotional freedom God intended for us to have. We move toward the life and purpose and wholeness He wants us to embrace. Let's start moving that direction.

1

Why We Have Emotions

*The highest dream we could ever dream, the wish that if
granted would make us happier than any other blessing,
is to know God, to actually experience him. The problem
is that we don't believe this idea is true. We assent to it
in our heads. But we don't feel it in our hearts.*

LARRY CRABB

G od created man in his own image, in the image of God he created
him, male and female he created them" (Genesis 1:27). Emotions are part of the package of blessing and inheritance that we receive
as humans. We are "fearfully and wonderfully made," as one writer of
the book of Psalms remarks. Our loving, living God didn't want to
shape us into unfeeling robots. This would've eliminated our privilege
of free will. It would've meant that when we expressed our committed
love and devotion to our Creator, it would be a programmed response
instead of a deeply held passion and sense of gratitude for the God who
made us, who knows how many hairs are on our heads, who knew us
before we were ever born.

God is emotional when it comes to His children. He, like any
good parents responding to the child they love, reveals His joy when
we are obedient and unveils His anger when we ignore His leading or
when we give ourselves over to the influence of anything outside of
Him and His best. Yes, He knows how our lives will unfold and how
many times we will repeat the same mistakes; nevertheless, I picture
Him pacing back and forth with anticipation and great love as He
awaits a prodigal son or daughter to return to the comfort and safety

15

of His arms. I see Him beaming with delight when His child, new to faith, takes her first steps in the direction of His leading. I see Him overcome by sorrow when He is holding us up during times of loss, illness, and pain.

Emotions Are a Gift

Emotions give our lives color, meaning, texture, and the ability to experience our journey deeply. They allow us to express our human experience to one another and to praise God from the depths of our hearts and souls. They help us convey the wave of energy that rises up in us as we experience the smile of a baby, the news of hardship, the toll of long-term struggle, the opportunity of our dreams, and the challenges and rewards of faith.

As I grew in my spiritual walk and matured as a person, I realized that my overly sensitive nature can be a gift if it is surrendered to the Lord. What I had once known only as weakness would eventually become a great strength for the purposes God had for my life. Compassion and mercy are the fruit of a more sensitive nature, and it comes naturally for me to intuitively pick up on the needs of others. When people are more sensitive, they tend to enjoy serving. They gravitate toward situations where they can nurture others. They are also very sensitive to their relationship with Christ—intuitively focused on pleasing Him, on serving Him, on fulfilling their purpose given by Him.

God can use your emotions for His glory, for the furthering of His kingdom. If you surrender negative emotions to Him and invest time managing and exploring your emotions, your life will be richer and more meaningful. But it has to become a choice in your life. We must learn not to rely on what we "feel" in the moment; instead, we need to learn to wait and evaluate why we feel certain things so that we can respond from a godly perspective.

This is not as easy as it sounds. And if anything, the people around us and the circumstances we are in tend to encourage emotional highs and lows. Friends who mean well can spur us on to ride the wave of emotions as they become invested in our current drama or our predicament. We can fuel each other out of a sense of interest or concern and not even realize we are elevating the risk of deadly emotions.

We all tend to react when we have someone attack us verbally, or when someone cuts us off on the freeway, or when we feel someone is crowding our space, or someone is threatening our job security. Even if I act on my feelings and respond positively, it may not be the best way to respond in the situation. A positive response could still lead to a negative outcome simply because sometimes "no response" is the best plan of action. When we wait, rather than react to a situation or to initial feelings, we have a better chance of getting the outcome God desires.

What I've been privileged to discover along the way is the truth about how emotions are a healthy, wonderful part of who we are as God's children and how some emotions, when left unchecked and untamed, can squelch life. They can actually consume our thinking, our belief, our trust, and our ability to live in God's abundance. This is where emotions take a turn from function to dysfunction. From uplifting to destructive. From life-giving to deadly.

What Controls Us?

Who or what is holding the remote control on your life? Think about that. What dictates your decisions, your whims, your actions, your moods, your willingness to help others, your desires, your need for boundaries, your inability or ability to set those boundaries? When we are in bondage to deadly emotions, the enemy is able to punch those buttons and trigger the worst outcome. And let's be honest here, we also do that to ourselves. The enemy can sit back and watch us self-destruct without lifting a finger. Left alone with our emotional baggage or out-of-control temperaments, we wander from the purpose of God and then completely miss the emotional freedom He longs for us to have. I've lived both sides of this, and I'm here to encourage you with the truth that this freedom from being controlled by emotions is worth fighting for, worth paying attention to, and worth the effort you're making right now to explore these intricacies in your heart and mind and spirit.

An important truth was revealed to me years ago when my oldest son, Josh, was about two years old. I couldn't take him anywhere without him throwing a tantrum. He wouldn't stay in his stroller at the mall and he didn't like to sit in a highchair at a restaurant, and so I'd stay home. It seemed easier than dealing with the humiliation and exhaustion of those public displays. The freedoms of my life seemed worth sacrificing because the cost of taking him anywhere was too much for me to bear. I know you're probably thinking, *Michelle, you needed to let that child know who is boss.* Remember, he was my first, so please go easy on me.

Thankfully I had a great friend named Sarah who had three kids a little older than mine. She was a strong and loving mom. I loved going over to her house because she seemed to be in control of everything. Her home felt peaceful and not overwhelmed by emotional turmoil like my home. She asked me one afternoon to meet her at the mall. You know what my answer was. "I can't. Josh won't stay in his stroller. He hates being at the mall." Can you imagine her tone when she answered, "What? Are you kidding? Michelle, you need to take him to the mall every day. And if he throws a tantrum you take him to the bathroom and spank his little bottom. You keep going to the mall until he stops doing that." I love it when people are so straight with me.

I took her advice and guess what? It worked! I went on several excursions with the new confidence that I could take control of my tantrum-prone toddler *and* I could change the situation for the better. After that I never had a problem going to the mall or anywhere else. And my Joshua is now a fine young man. If it were not for Sarah, I may have continued living with frustration and helplessness, especially as Josh became older. If I hadn't taken her advice, I would've had a spoiled child on my hands, and all the rest of my children would most likely be spoiled too. And think how limited my life would be. I would've told God "no" when He asked me to go places because I was too worried about sparking an incident. God can't use or direct someone who is always hiding from life or from the possible next step.

When we experience an emotion spiraling out of control, it is like a spoiled child wanting his way—only it's our flesh crying out, not a child. Our flesh cries out for what it wants, and when we continue to give in to its demands, we remain in bondage and forfeit the hope of living a healthy life of emotional freedom. As long as those emotions are controlling us and we're not fully submitted to Christ, we will feel miserable, depressed, anxious, guilty, shameful, angry, fearful, and insecure. It is our choice to follow God's advice and wisdom, just as it was my choice to take Sarah's advice and follow her mentoring lead. God has given us the tools to overcome the trials of the flesh, but we have to embrace His ways and not continue to give in to the desires of the flesh.

Personality, Behaviors, and Emotions

Serious. Silly. Type A. Free-spirited. Take charge. Behind the scenes. Controlled. No matter which personality or personal approaches to life we have, we are all emotional. There isn't one type of person or character who gets to claim they are emotion-free (though some will try, which we'll discuss). While many of us may have tried to rid ourselves of feeling emotions, this is not what God intends as a solution to overcoming deadly emotions. Ignoring or squelching all emotion would make us cold, distant, and definitely not open to intimacy.

For those of us who show our emotions more than others, this news is great news...it's freedom! But don't stop reading here. All of us, whether we wear our emotions on our sleeves or hold them close to our hearts, need to come to the place of allowing God to help us get ahold of negative, dangerous emotions and bring them under the lordship of Jesus Christ. Do you recognize when your emotions are getting out of control? Do you ever feel frustrated about decisions made as a result of reacting to a situation too quickly? We have all been there, believe me.

How many times have you responded with regrettable statements or actions when someone hurt you or talked about you behind your back? Or you've misread a situation or a friend's comment and turned up the volume on your rage or jealousy? We've all made decisions based on feelings instead of what God wants from us at the moment. Feelings will lie to us, deceive us, and that is why it's so important to learn what God's Word says about these potentially destructive forces in our lives.

The Internally Explosive Person

We must remember that what we hide still has power
over us, but when we bring things out in the open,
they begin losing their grip immediately.

JOYCE MEYER, *MANAGING YOUR EMOTIONS*

"The truth will set us free" (John 8:32). In her book *Managing Your Emotions,* speaker and author Joyce Meyer stresses the importance of being honest when you are feeling down or moving toward negative emotions. It helps others know it's not about them. I tend to try to keep quiet when I am feeling a lot of negative emotions. I used to suppress them so that I wouldn't emotionally explode or do something I might regret. Most often I tend to be volatile during a certain time of the month (Can you relate?). Now I try to acknowledge these fleeting emotions and deal with them. And if I do explode when one of my kids doesn't do a chore or when someone negates something I care about, I acknowledge the rise of the anger or the sense of pride or whatever it is. I then apologize and keep myself honest.

I went with a new friend to lunch one day, and she began describing her personality using words like "unemotional" and "solid." She went on to say how she is usually quite calm in situations that would trigger most women to become highly emotional.

Okay, there are a lot of these people out there who claim they are unaffected by the types of situations or moods that influence others. But there is usually something else going on. There is usually a truth behind such self-imposed stoicism. This was the case with my friend.

After a while she admitted that being forced as a child to shield her heart from the rejection and verbal abuse of her parents had caused her to shut down emotionally and lose touch with her truest feelings. While her personality is rather introverted, it was clear that these experiences from her childhood and wounds from her recent past were the real reasons that she kept her emotions locked up tight.

You see, she wasn't an unemotional person. She would most likely be considered an introvert, yes, but the emotions were there, boiling below the surface. No one knew because she came across as calm, quiet, and collected. Her version of "calm" really was about remaining a safe distance from anything or anyone that could hurt her. She'd learned this response.

I'm sure you've heard the story about the frog that willingly stays in a pot of water as he is being boiled alive. This example is so relevant to our emotional shielding and self-protection that I want to reiterate it. When the frog first gets thrown into a pot of cool tap water, which is resting on a soon-to-be activated stove burner, he is completely unaware of his destiny. He, like any frog in water, is happy and content swimming around. He has no idea that his situation is about to change. As the water slowly heats up, the frog is still unaware, splashing around, occasionally lifting his head above the water line to see his surroundings. The process is slow; he doesn't detect each small rise in temperature. Nevertheless, the change is occurring and pretty soon it will all be over for the poor little frog. It isn't until the water is at a full-throttle boil that the frog realizes that life as he's known it is over. He is cooked and frog legs are served up with a side dish of asparagus. (No, I didn't test this illustration to see if it is factual.)

Calm, collected introverts or unemotional people may hold their feelings close to their chests, and like the frog in the slow warming water, allow their feelings to slowly heat up over time until suddenly they are boiling inside. When another person irritates those old wounds or triggers former emotional hot spots, suddenly the "calm" person is overcome by these emotions and even surprised by them. They have ignored the low-level emotions for so long that they feel bombarded by these strange sensations and aren't able to process them. The person who incited these emotions wonders what in the world happened. When emotions left simmering on the burner hit that boiling point…stand back!

People Pleasers

The compassionate person responds to the needs of others. The empathetic person relates to the needs of others. But the people pleaser tries to *second guess, juggle,* and *protect* the emotional needs of others. Considering that most of us aren't even sure how to discern our own emotions, the idea of trying to protect or sidestep the emotions of others to avoid causing problems is almost humorous…and most often disastrous. Many of us fall into this category. We sacrifice our own well-being, purpose, opinions, and leading to please people who come at us from the right and left. We're often ignoring God's voice from above.

There's nothing wrong with working hard to please our families, our spouses, our bosses, our coworkers, our church families, and others who are connected to us. But if we ignore our true feelings over and over because we're fearful of people or their potential responses, nothing is ever resolved. And we are never honest with ourselves or others. When we shut our emotions completely off due to pain, heart bruises from our past, fear of people, or even because our personality is more prone to do so, God has to open our eyes so we'll see our denial. He has to reactivate those places in our hearts that have dried up from lack of attention, air, and nurturing. Without this help, those negatives play a part in altering our ability to truly feel all God intended for us to feel: to love deeply, to have intimate relationships, to experience deep friendship, and to have joy in experiencing the freedom He speaks of in His Word.

The Externally Explosive Person

We all have our moments of emotional outbursts, but there are those who allow their emotions to completely control every moment, often triggering reactions to almost everything that offends them. This is usually a result of behavior learned while growing up or an internal stress thermometer that is out of whack. It's one thing to watch a two-year-old throw a tantrum, but it's quite another when you see an adult explode all over the clerk at the grocery store over incorrect change. I see this behavior more and more as our society becomes a boiling pot of extreme pressures.

There is little excuse for exploding all over people when we feel hurt or angry, but unless we truly submit our lack of self-control to God, it may feel next to impossible to change this cycle of behavior. Peace comes from hearing the Word of God and from meditation in prayer. Prayer and the hearing of God's Word are the first steps to calming the fiery furnace that burns inside. When we are overloaded in our responsibilities, when we are stretched beyond imagination in our personal lives, how else can we exercise self-control?

I've learned to detect when I am getting to the point of overload. I work very hard to keep the stresses of everyday life out of my home in order to make it a haven of peace for my family. Occasionally the stress of juggling the personal lives of my kids triggers my explosive behavior. When they all need to be somewhere at a certain time, and I need to be at an appointment, and dinner still needs to be put on the stove, I feel myself getting angry. Unless I take action, it's not long before I'm yelling at the kids and anyone who comes across my path. The best thing is for me to avoid situations where I feel this overwhelmed and give myself a chance at sanity and my family a chance at unity.

It's not the end of the world if the kids can't go to every event or participate in every sport. Sometimes we are so focused on making up for what we didn't have we deprive our kids of the very thing they need…peace. I've also learned some practical solutions. If I know I have a heavy day ahead, I may put dinner on in the morning so all I have to do is come home and serve it. Also, to avoid feeling as if I'm going to explode at the next person who crosses me in some way, I make sure my spiritual and personal life is in order. God is a God of order, and sometimes as believers it's easy for us to think that His job is to pick up the messes we've caused.

The Lord cares about our growth and challenges us to mature throughout His Word. When we submit ourselves to a life of order, peace comes in our homes and our hearts. When we come to the place where we accept changes in plans, learn to accept that not everything will always fall perfectly into place, understand we may have to wait patiently in line, or relax when we get caught in traffic on the way home—we will begin to feel peace instead of turmoil. There will always be out-of-control moments, and in those times we must lay our idea of perfection aside and accept change, failures, and disappointments.

Do you tend to explode all the time? Ask yourself these questions:

1. How is my exploding changing my situation?
2. How does my behavior impact others?
3. What is really going on inside of me?
4. Am I angry at the person or with myself?
5. What are some ways I can add order to my life and get help?

These are just a few questions that will help you get on the path to self-control. Abusing others because we haven't instituted peace in our disordered world is not what God intended.

> Thanks be to God, who gives us the victory through our Lord
> Jesus Christ (1 Corinthians 15:57).

Do these people we've been talking about sound familiar? Our personalities, heart bruises, self-protection, fear, and desire to please people instead of God can cause us to react strongly to situations. What I hope you glean from this book is the ability to respond in a way that is glorifying to others and to God. When we allow deadly emotions to control us, we are setting ourselves up for ruined marriages, friendships, families, jobs, and so on. We won't thrive and experience all God has for us.

Deadly Emotion Is the Enemy's Counterfeit

God's plan for us, His desire for us, is to live in peace, joy, and victory. He wants us to be set free from emotional bondage that destroys what He is building in us and through us. When we feel controlled by the seven deadly emotions—fear, jealousy, lust, anger, stress, shame, and pride—we often blame others, our personalities, our upbringing, or even God for making us this way. But the real reason those emotions are controlling us is because we haven't surrendered this area of our lives completely to God. Instead, we are giving ourselves over to the enemy's counterfeit responses. It's so easy for our emotions to quickly take us from a place of light to a place of darkness. If you're buying into the counterfeit life, you're not living the authentic, God-centered one.

By God's grace we are given a way to counter the counterfeits! The truths in God's Word are the keys to unlocking the freedom we so desire. Learning how emotions control us and understanding the lies we are deceived by will empower us to work out our emotions in a way that brings victory to our lives instead of destruction.

How much greater would it be if our responses led to a place of victory instead of a place of sinful behavior? The feeling of being out of control is similar to the feeling we get when we drop 15 feet from the highest peak of a roller coaster. Our stomachs feel as if they dropped to our feet, our minds spin with confusion, and just when we feel we have recovered and are soaring toward more positive heights, here comes the next big drop. But unlike the roller-coaster scenario, in life we don't see the next big drop coming up. We move along and everything is just fine. We could even be on top of the world…and then we get a phone call, we hear a story, we get a negative response from someone, and we are in a dark place, a depressed state, and we react with anger, jealousy, or fear. When we are headed for a dark response, we immediately need to take our thoughts captive and shed the light of truth on them. God reveals His truth to us in His Word. This is where the freedom lies.

> We destroy arguments and every lofty opinion raised against
> the knowledge of God, and take every thought captive to
> obey Christ, being ready to punish every disobedience, when
> your obedience is complete (2 Corinthians 10:5).

Once we learn how to use God's Word as a source of truth against the emotions that hold us captive, we are able to walk in victory rather than remain victims. Why am I staying depressed for days because Sally was mean to me or my boss didn't affirm me? Why do I fall into a state of despair after I make a mistake? Why do I allow jealousy to destroy my relationships? Why am I up and down in my emotions?

Situations may seem unredeemable, like we've hit a dead end. But there is nothing we can't overcome with Christ's strength. Nothing! And with the right tools we will be on our way to a new place of growth in our lives.

Deadly Emotions Disguised

It says in 1 Peter 5:8 that "the devil prowls around like a roaring lion, seeking someone to devour." He has come to kill, steal, and destroy, but I don't think that most people really understand how Satan attacks us *behind* the walls of our minds and hearts. If he can work his way into our minds, he can affect us where it hurts the most…our way of interpreting, sensing, seeing, and responding to the world and our circumstances. As rational and logical as we like to come across to others, most of us are controlled by what we feel, not by what we think.

Emotions that have gone awry are far more dangerous than more obvious outward sin because they can go for years without being detected or managed. We write off the emotions as legitimate responses because of our mood, situation, or energy. Have you ever used "I'm sorry, it's just that I'm so tired" as your catchall excuse for bad behavior or an outburst? We may think we're fooling the outside world and maybe we even manage to fool ourselves, but the real trouble is brewing in our private world where God sees us and knows us.

Deadly emotions can be tucked away in the shadows of our strengths. I am sensitive, and the manifestation of sensitivity emerges in the form of service, compassion, and care, but the deadly emotions lurking in the shadows are fear and pride. My worry about the needs of others leads me to be "a rescuer." Rescuing people doesn't sound so bad, but when we rescue someone we are trying to take on God's job. God doesn't require you or me to be Him. As a new believer I wanted to save everyone. Over time I realized that God is the only One who saves, and I have to point people to Him, not to me. Pointing people to me would be a way of getting attention and feeding my pride. Consider how closely your actions are intertwined with your driving needs and deadly emotions. Think of times in the past week when you have tried to serve the deadly emotions instead of using the strengths God has given to you to serve Him.

Let's examine how we currently deal with deadly emotions (or how we don't deal with them) so that we are willing and able to let God direct us to the path of freedom.

2

How We Deal with Emotions

Mark is driving down I-25 going 70 miles an hour. This is one of those days when everything that could go wrong does. Exhausted from the late night before, he awoke to the jarring sound of the garbage truck loading right outside his window. *Why so early?* he thought. *They don't usually pick up until after eight.* Suddenly it hits him! He's late for his 8:30 meeting. He jumps up, looks at his wife in her blissful wonderland, leans over and kisses her lightly on the cheek, and makes his way to the shower. He can just imagine how bothered his clients will be if they are waiting in the office lobby and he walks in late. And there will be no time to catch up after the meeting because his secretary scheduled nonstop appointments for the rest of the day.

Already frazzled, Mark showers, throws on his clothes, and runs a comb quickly through his hair as he races out the door. He won't have time to eat or even get his much-needed morning coffee. Maybe, just maybe, he will make it in time to slip into his office before his clients arrive. Once in the car, he glances at the gas gauge and finds the tank on empty. Sarah used his car the night before to take the kids to all their activities and didn't refuel. "Geez!" he shouts as he hits the steering wheel with the palms of both hands. He screeches out the driveway and heads for the closest gas station. He hopes things get better.

Unfortunately the rest of Mark's day is a continuous onslaught of mishaps and irritations. Finally, at 10:00, he is on his way home after a day of poring over contracts and seeing clients. He's exhausted, bleary-eyed, and has barely had a moment to catch his breath all day. When he calls to tell Sarah he is on his way, she is upset because he is late coming home again. The rest of the drive he anticipates the mood that awaits him when he walks through the front door of his house. Sarah is going to slam him up and down for being late. It's all he's thinking about when suddenly a car pulls out in front of him, almost causing him to run off the road. Normally this would be no big deal, but Mark has had it. He steps on the gas to catch up to the guy who cut him off. It takes him a while and a speed of 90 mph, but finally he gets right beside the vehicle that cut him off. He rolls down his window, screams at the top of his lungs "What the heck are you doing?" shakes his fist, and moves his car in close. He suddenly slows down to get ahold of himself. He'd lost it. Why?

This is definitely a situational response. And while Mark seems to overreact while on the highway, he is no different than the millions of people who are living in a constant state of overload caused by stress from their day and the feeling that at any moment they'll explode. Mark is not an evil guy. He doesn't typically struggle with anger issues, and he's known to all who live and work with him as a tenderhearted and compassionate man. But in his "situational response," Mark could've caused his family a great expense...Mark's life. What if the person he pulled up to had a gun? What if Mark lost control of his car? What if he hit the car and killed or injured someone else?

Deadly emotion produces toxic behavior that can lead to serious consequences. Can you relate? Maybe you don't experience the burst of road rage that Mark did, but instead, you hold all that work stress in until you get home and erupt like a volcano all over your family. We all lose our composure more than we want to admit, especially as Christians. We mistakenly want to think that because we are Christians we are immune to deadly emotions. Yes, we will experience these emotions, but as believers we have Christ living in us and His power to overcome situational responses and very bad days.

When we face the same situations, we can either act out in our emotional state as Mark did or we can respond in a way God would want us to. *Responding* instead of reacting is so critical to the success of overcoming in this area of our lives. When you react, your base emotions rise to the forefront without a filter. However, when you respond in God's strength, you're able to monitor, soften, or squelch those destructive behaviors. The good news is that the more you immerse yourself in God's Word and love, the more immediate your godly responses will be. It takes God's strength and peace to override those knee-jerk reactions that can get us and others into patterns of harmful behavior.

Heart Bruises

Many people fail to understand the ways their histories impact their adult lives, or how their choices in people, repetitive situations, and decisions today—even their emotional reactions—are connected to early negative experiences.

DR. LAURA SCHLESSINGER
BAD CHILDHOOD—GOOD LIFE

Most of us have no idea how and why we react to life the way we do. We sift through our difficulties never actually focusing on what causes our reactions, answers, and decisions. We react to something and then think, *Why did I say that?* And most often those strong emotions are a reaction to something said or done by the people closest to us. Our family members or dear friends can often trigger our negative emotions because they know the most about us. They are frequently tied to our past or intimately acquainted with our struggles. And they are our most constant reminders of our past heart bruises.

When a heart bruise is subconsciously triggered, a well of emotion comes up inside me. It is nearly physical. Something they have said to me or something they have done is linked to an automatic expression of one of the following emotions: fear, shame, guilt, humiliation, or pride. I feel threatened, almost smothered by the comment or action, and my reaction can be harsh if I don't take a moment to think it through and then respond. This requires me to be introspective, to stop and process what was said. It also requires me to give the person who said it the benefit of the doubt. Most people don't want to hurt us. And if we always turn our attention back to the other person, we never discover more about ourselves and our feelings. Our path to healing requires us to first recognize how *we've* been processing emotions. What patterns do we fall into? How do we hide our feelings or hide from them? Identify which of the following methods you've relied on to protect yourself from feeling those heart bruises, and then we'll explore God's ways.

Avoidance of any negative feelings. This method keeps us safe from conflict and enables us to avoid confrontation. If we can avoid situations and people that pose a threat of any kind, we can stay clear of dealing with the emotions they trigger. For example, if you know your husband is going to be angry with you when he gets home, and you leave the house and go shopping, this keeps you temporarily safe. You've built in this avoidance action so that by the time you get home he will be past his anger and you won't have to deal with the issues underlying his anger or your denial.

Many relationships end up stuck at this protective, surface level where both parties avoid facing any confrontation that could turn into a serious argument or a breakthrough. I heard a well-known comedian make a joke out of avoiding his wife, stating that if guys will learn a few key phrases it will keep things cool at home. His premise was that if men respond with phrases like "Uh huh," "Is that right?" and look up every once in a while, women will feel like they were heard and it will keep the peace at home. Pretty funny! There is some truth to it, but the only problem is that while this may be the key to a peaceful relationship, it's certainly not the key to intimacy.

Suppressing and denying feelings. You've heard the saying "Never let them see you sweat." Whether we planned to or not, many of us have adopted this as a motto for life. We learn along the way that it is better to not let others see us become emotional or express our emotions. Some of us learn this within our families because we're told not to reveal emotions. Others train themselves because of education or workplace standards and high expectations that dictate behavior: If you're afraid, don't let anyone know it. If you're anxious, make sure to hide it.

Subconsciously or consciously stuffing our emotions is a very common way to deal with life. While denying feelings seems to keep us safe, it is actually keeping us from strong relationships and authentic living. If we pretend to ourselves and others that we really aren't feeling down, discouraged, upset, or afraid, we somehow think these feelings aren't part of our experience. But those feelings do indeed exist and are brewing below the surface, interrupting our lives periodically when they erupt.

Using the gender defense. The "Girls are emotional, boys aren't" comment is more than a fallback stereotype. It becomes an easy excuse for men to distance themselves from emotions and for women to dismiss their reactions as gender mandated.

My sons are always saying about their sister, "Madison is just being emotional; she's too sensitive." Madison may appear to be more emotional (just like her mom) or maybe she has reacted negatively and more passionately than they would, but it doesn't make my boys less emotional than their sister. And young boys using this cliché against their sisters is not the only example of using the gender excuse. I'll bet that you or a close friend of yours has used it somewhat recently. I'd say that next to the "I'm tired" excuse for being overly dramatic, the next common excuse women use—whether we state it out loud or not—is the "I'm female" theory. It is a way we let ourselves off the hook from looking at why we respond to words, people, or situations in certain ways.

Inclination toward emotional expression, outbursts, or acknowledgment is less subject to gender and more related to personality, upbringing, background, and the heart bruise history of our lives. There are men and women who struggle to express emotion or who allow emotions more control and influence in their lives than they do God.

Shifting blame. Of all the ways we attempt to ignore the power of deadly emotions over us, perhaps the most common is by denying personal responsibility. We emotionally respond in ways that are unacceptable and blame it on the shortcomings of others. It's so easy—and convenient!—to shift blame to someone else. The ol' saying "The devil made me do it" can temporarily shift the spotlight off ourselves, but eventually God's truth will shed light on our truth—we need change in our lives.

When God is dealing with our inner sanctuary, we need to allow ourselves to see mistakes, trials, and failures as part of spiritual growth instead of an attack on our personality. Undertanding the importance of actually looking at our own "stuff" and working through it is the beginning of a powerful spiritual journey. The enemy wants you to keep blaming him for all your problems because it means you'll never start growing. None of us wants to admit when we blow it. Pride can be much greater than our desire to grow, and it does really come before a fall. Eventually we'll face the loss of a relationship, job, opportunity, chance to embrace our purpose…and run out of excuses or people to burden with the responsibility of our problems. We'll have to shift the focus of blame back to ourselves.

It makes sense that we resort to these excuses, modes of denial, and avoidance tactics. Along with how to color inside the lines and print the alphabet, we probably learned self-preservation from kindergarten onward. In our situation example with Mark's bad day, he had likely suppressed his feelings throughout his day as a way of coping. He probably felt he couldn't tell Sarah she should've filled the gas tank up the night before because he feels responsible to do those things for her. He couldn't get overly mad about the alarm clock because it was just one of those things. He couldn't get angry about not taking a lunch break or having a moment to himself throughout his day because busy days are good for business.

Where does God fit into the picture of our emotional health? Where does what He says in His Word impact the way we act out our feelings? Feelings are natural responses to what happens to us. But handling feelings with no grounding in God's principles are the beginnings of deadly emotions—ones that bring forth actions that can be destructive to our spiritual journey as well as our everyday living. So how do we even begin this journey to emotional freedom? As we examine the seven deadly emotions, we'll explore:

- testimonials of people who have overcome deadly emotions
- the root of each deadly emotion
- biblical examples of emotions
- the lies we believe
- biblical truths
- deadly consequences
- how to become life-givers
- the fruit of the Spirit and emotional freedom

Emotional Freedom

I once heard this quote and never forgot it: "One of life's greatest tragedies is to go to your grave with your music still in you." Our Lord wants to play a beautiful symphony through all of us, but because of all the hurts and the scars that bind many of us, by the time the music comes out, it's not very pleasant to listen to. *God* wants to heal us, to free us from emotional bondage, so we can get our melody out to others around us.

So as we work through the seven deadly emotions—fear, jealousy, anger, lust, shame, stress, and pride—we will begin to experience the wonderful freedom God longs to give us. The person who is able to surrender deadly emotions and no longer be controlled by them has peace.

3

The Face of Fear

Fear not, for I am with you; be not dismayed, for I
am your God; I will strengthen you, I will help you,
I will uphold you with my righteous right hand.

ISAIAH 41:10

I vividly recall strolling down the streets of my neighborhood, staring up at the trees shadowing over me, protecting me from the blazing sun. I remember all the wonderful things most kids remember, like the jingle of the ice cream truck from far off and all of us scrambling to scrape together enough change to get our favorite flavor. I recall endless summer nights playing ball in the streets until Mom would call us in as we begged to stay out a little bit longer. Those are memories of the good things that brought peace to my daily life. But my memories of nightfall aren't as bright.

As a young girl with a strong imagination, fear had me in its grasp. I would lie down in bed as fear worked its way into my mind and tormented me until finally, exhausted, I would drift to sleep. Shadows on the wall became evil people; noises in the house signaled someone coming to get me. Or so I thought. As I got older, my childhood fears were replaced with different ones—the same demons just different faces. The mere thought of being alone was one of my greatest fears. I was afraid of interacting with people. Afraid someone wouldn't like me or understand me. Afraid of rejection or hurting someone else's feelings. Trying to manage my fear was exhausting, but it became my way of life.

Once I accepted Christ, I began to walk the journey of overcoming fear. I knew fear was keeping me from so many things God had for me. I desperately wanted to be free of it once and for all. At night when I couldn't sleep because of worries, I would say the name of Jesus over and over until peace would cover me and I would fall asleep. Sometimes I would be so exhausted from lack of sleep it was hard to function during the day.

I was living on my own at 20 years old, and fear was a haunting, familiar presence standing between me and the purpose God had for my life. As I overcame one fear, God would work with me on another.

Fear's Legacy

My mom also experienced fears growing up, and hers were even more paralyzing. At age 20, she went to the hospital with an ulcer. But the roots of her fears went much deeper. Her father was an alcoholic who feared abandonment, rejection, and was in a continual state of paranoia over most areas of his life. He'd been abused by his father growing up and had believed his father's and the enemy's lie that he was worthless. So as an adult man, he would rant and rave in front of his family nightly. He physically abused my grandmother, my mom, and her siblings. There were nights my mother would wake up to her dad pulling her out of her bed by her hair and dragging her down the hall while yelling shameful things at her. My grandfather died at age 42, destroyed by alcohol, but the pain and suffering as a result of his horrible abuse would be part of my mom's family for years to come.

The fears that were planted in my mother's heart from her horrible childhood stayed with her. I remember her bracing the ironing board against the door at night for extra security when I was young. Once my mom came to know Christ, there was a huge division among her brothers and sister. Though Mom's mother had a religious background, she wasn't serving the Lord, which was hard for my mom. She underwent a lot of persecution from the family. One time we stayed at my grandmother's while my parents were ministering at a church nearby. During the entire visit my grandmother acted very hatefully toward my mom and barely said a word. We were going to endure this for two weeks because we had no other place to stay, and my parents didn't have the money to leave. My mom ended up selling her sewing machine so we had the money to leave earlier than planned.

Even after Mom knew Christ and her life changed radically, it still took many years for her to overcome the extreme fear she'd lived with for so long. She did it by reciting the Word of God and dispelling the lies she believed for so long. Lies such as, "You are not important," "You are not loved," "You are not accepted," and "You will never be anything in this life" were replaced with God's truth using her name. "For God so loved [Sandy], that he gave his only Son, that whoever believes in him should not perish but have eternal life" (John 3:16). "If God is for [Sandy], who can be against [her]?" (Romans 8:31). "But when the kindness and love of God our Savior appeared, he saved [Sandy], not because of righteous things [she] had done, but because of his mercy" (Titus 3:4-5 NIV).

Mom stated Scripture's truths to keep from giving herself over to the fears of not being a good mother or a good wife or not pleasing God. And we allow fear to poison us and keep us in captivity. I was afraid I'd failed God and would never have children. I feared I would die young. When I had children, I feared I would not be a good mom. As my children got older, I feared for their lives. Like my mom, I had to start countering my fear-filled thoughts with the Word of God.

My mom's relationship with Christ was the beginning of hope for the rest of her family, but it would be 15 years before they would follow in her steps. During those years my mother endured their taunts, humiliation, and great rejection, but she always forgave, always loved. Once, after a round of severe rejection from my grandmother, my mom felt the Lord speak to her heart about washing her mother's feet. She didn't want to do this, but she worked against her feelings and followed through. Something bad broke in their relationship afterward. It was the beginning of God opening the heart of my granny and softening her so she could be open to God doing a work of healing in her heart.

The change in her was beautiful to behold. Not only did my granny come to know the Lord, but her transformation led all my mom's siblings to Christ as well. Few of us could be as patient and forgiving as my mom was toward her mother. Mom taught me perseverance through her actions.

My mom could have justified cutting all of her family out of her life and staying angry with them. But the consequences would've been a hardened heart and indifference to those she held dear. Instead she chose to follow a way that provided a legacy of hope. Her actions would teach her children a great lesson of faith. There are five kids in my family, and all of us understand the power of forgiveness and grace for people, especially for those who don't know Christ.

The Root of Fear

Do the fears I've talked about sound familiar? Are you afraid to be alone? Are you afraid you won't be a good parent? Do you constantly have a shadow of fear that you or someone close to you will die? As we move through the difficult journey of dealing with deadly emotions, we will be enlightened many times about the influence of fear and the importance of addressing it with God's peace and promises. Starting the exploration of deadly emotions with "fear" is deliberate. As you'll discover, fear is often the primary emotion behind many of the other deadly emotions we'll tackle. Understanding how fear takes root in our lives and how God has power over our personal fears, will enable us to face and overcome the other emotions that keep us struggling, stagnant, or sinful.

We notice most fears initially when they creep into our minds as irrational thoughts that are either an exaggeration of a truth or an outright lie. If we aren't equipped to battle these thoughts, the enemy has an opportunity to keep us ineffective for God. What are some of your greatest fears? Have you asked yourself if they are founded on truths or on lies? Have they kept you from doing things you desire to do? From what you feel called to do? It's time you step out into all God has for you. It isn't easy to face fears, but God is with you. He showed me how to do it and how to trust Him instead of trusting in myself or my fears. And He's allowing me to help you!

Before we go on, take a moment and list all your fears. We'll come back to your list in a moment.

God Is Bigger Than Your Circumstances

In the book of Deuteronomy, God instructs the Israelites not to be concerned when they go into battle and see a massive army greater than they are. He assures them that He will be with them and reminds them He is the One who has always taken care of them: "Hear, O Israel: Today you are on the verge of battle with your enemies. Do not let your heart faint, do not be afraid, and do not tremble or be terrified because of them; for the LORD your God is He who goes with you, to fight for you against your enemies, to save you" (20:3-4 NKJV).

Oh, how we so easily forget the One who goes with us into battle, the One who is our advocate, our defense against our enemies. Do not be afraid, for you have the Lord on your side! We are reminded again when Jesus came walking on the water toward the disciples while they were in the boat fishing. Peter got out of the boat to walk toward Jesus. Suddenly he looked around and saw the wind and became afraid. He immediately began to sink and cried out to Jesus to save him. Jesus saved him, but He also rebuked him saying, "Why are you afraid, O you of little faith?" (Matthew 8:26). Why did Peter suddenly become fearful? He looked at his circumstances and no longer believed. How often is our unbelief a result of us looking around at our circumstances? We see obstacles, we notice how other people are doing things differently, and we clearly notice our flaws and past failures. And we sink. We do need to recognize our circumstances, but when we dwell on them, when our thoughts become focused on the impossibilities instead of the possibilities, we are going to get afraid and like Peter we will sink in our fear.

Why We're Afraid

Fully-developed love expels every particle of fear, for fear always contains some of the torture of feeling guilty (1 John 4:18 PHILLIPS).

What we tend to fear most is what we don't understand. We fear death because it is foreign to us, we fear relationships because they are unpredictable, and we fear flying because we have to believe that something beyond ourselves and beyond our comfort zone is responsible for our safety. What God wants us to believe in each of these circumstances is that we can trust Him. No matter what trials we face, no matter what detours come our way, He is here and He will deliver us from calamity. Out of the miry clay He takes us and sets our feet upon a rock. He says through the apostle Paul, "Finally, brothers, whatever is true, whatever is honorable, whatever is just, whatever is pure, whatever is lovely, whatever is commendable, if there is any excellence, if there is anything worthy of praise, think about these things. What you have learned and received and heard and seen in me—practice these things, and the God of peace will be with you" (Philippians 4:8-9).

So where does the peace come from? Where does the freedom from fear really begin? It begins in walking out the truths in God's Word. It begins with dwelling on and living out what is pure and holy in our lives. It begins in thinking on and acting on what is honorable, lovely, and commendable. When we live any other way, fear turns to anxiousness and anxiousness turns to stress. We live in a pretty stressed out society. How much of our stress is determined by our fears?

I've realized that over the years my fear has involved much more than my feelings. It involved my mind, thought life, and even impacted my body. Fear is a paralyzing force.

Inherited Fear—Connie's Story

When you meet Connie you are immediately drawn in by her humor and strong sense of self. The first thing you notice is her heritage—her dark tresses and strong accent and bold personality announce she is Italian. She is all about spreading love to those around her with her charm. But being Italian wasn't the only thing passed down to Connie.

The day I met with Connie we sat in a quaint downtown restaurant in Franklin, Tennessee. Before we got down to business she had me laughing. One way Connie has learned to cope with some of her trials in life is through humor. She shared the sequence of childhood memories that for so long affected her ability to have faith and caused an ongoing battle with fear.

Fear goes along with worrying. We worry because we're afraid something terrible is going to happen. Life, like the stock market, has its ups and downs. We worry because of the unknown about what will happen to our children, our finances, or our aging parents. If we're single, we worry about who is going to take care of us. If we are married, we wonder, "What if my husband leaves?" These are fears I've dealt with.

I grew up with an alcoholic father who wanted me to be his little protégé. I am the oldest, and the oldest takes the biggest bullet—at least it worked that way in my family. I was so afraid I wouldn't please my dad, and I wanted him to be proud of me. For many years this fear of failure kept me from stepping out and trying anything.

Growing up in an Italian family was great. We had a lot of fun and, of course, we had great food all the time. But I grew up surrounded by a bunch of worrywarts. Whatever the normal family does, Italians do it times two. We are so emotional and exaggerative, so everything is a much bigger deal. And when it came to worrying, we worried over everything. And when I say everything...I mean everything.

I remember bringing my newborn, Amy, over to see my parents. I'd placed little booties on her feet, and my mother saw them and said, "Oh my gosh, those booties are too tight. You're going to cut off her circulation!" And she grabbed Amy's feet and pulled the booties off as if Amy's life were at risk. Everything was catastrophic drama. You'd think a family of such big personalities would be fearful of nothing. I don't fear talking to a crowd of 10,000 people because if there's one thing we learned in our home, it was how to talk. But guess what? I am afraid of water. My parents couldn't swim so none of us learned to swim. There are four of us kids, and we all have tremendous fear of the water. I purposely have made it a point to nip this particular fear in the bud with my kids. I put them in swimming lessons when they were young. It sounds like such a little thing, but when you're near water and are afraid you could drown, it's not so little.

Fear and worry are the greatest demons I've dealt with in my life. I'm still working through the worrying. I struggle every day. The worries have changed over the years because my fears have changed, but they are always here. I'm afraid of flying, but I still fly. The airlines would probably rather I gave in to my fears and stayed home because I'm worried the entire time I'm on the plane. The whole time I'm wishing that I were the pilot and in control of the plane. But guess what? I'd be too afraid to get a license. Every time my kids or I get on a flight, I pray for everyone who has something to do with the aircraft: the maintenance people, the air traffic controllers, flight attendants, the pilot, the co-pilot. The list goes on and on.

I have so many memories of fear-related remarks my parents have made. Once when I was en route with my girls from Des Moines, Iowa, to Chicago to see my parents, Dad told me to call and check in with him after I'd driven for an hour. When I didn't call him after exactly one hour, he called me and asked, "What happened? In my mind I had you splattered all over the road. Are you all right?" When fear is controlling you, everything is such a huge deal. Fear robs you of joy in life and debilitates you from becoming all you can be. I didn't want to pass along such a legacy to my daughters. Anytime I'm afraid when my daughters are swimming or getting on a plane, I try not to show it. I want them to feel the peace and security that I rarely felt as a child.

God's Truth for the Lies of Fear

Here are a few of the fears most of us struggle with and some truths to combat them.

Lie #1: I'm the only one dealing with these sins and struggles. Fear makes us feel lonely and alone in our trial. We separate ourselves from other people so they don't catch on to our problems. Do you sometimes believe that you're the only one in your circle, in your church, in your community who struggles with your particular trial or sin?

The truth: All of us struggle with the same thoughts. Some are just able to overcome them better than others. Nobody is immune to feelings of insecurity or fear of rejection. We all struggle with sin and fight the enemy's use of temptation. Everyone has bad thoughts—some we are ashamed to even admit. But they are just thoughts, and the enemy will always be working to move those thoughts into action in our lives. If we were to display all our thoughts and past failures before the world, we'd be surprised at how similar they are to other people's experiences.

Lie # 2: If people know me, they'll reject me. We have learned to believe that if people know us, if they know we aren't perfect, if they know we struggle with sin, if they know our insecurities, they will cast us off.

The truth: What if we open up to someone and they don't like us? Not everyone will like us, and we will at some point experience rejection. But we are already accepted by the One who loves us like no other, and while we do want to be accepted by others, we can be at peace knowing God fully accepts us for who we are. If God is the only one we are trying please, and we are truly God crazy and focused on what He thinks and what He desires, what other people think of us is unimportant. Our security and our peace come from our relationship with Him. You'll be surprised at how many people will be drawn to you once they see this peace in your life and when they see that you're not looking to be made complete by the opinions or adoration of others.

Lie #3: If I keep things the same, I'm safe. How many of us try to control every little thing in order to make sure there are no surprises? We can become so afraid of the unknown that we're unable to walk in the things God has for us. Both of these taken to the extreme are debilitating and paralyzing, keeping us from really growing in our faith or toward a future.

The truth: God is all about change. Don't be afraid of it; embrace it! When we are afraid of change in our lives, it's because we dread loss of control. This is exactly where Christ wants us—at the point of surrendering our grip on every aspect of our lives so He can take it and shape it. As much as I'd like to think life is better when I'm in control, I'm the first to admit that the times when God brought *His* perfect order to replace my chaos were beautiful. This is the way He is glorified. This is the way our faith is built. If things stay the same, how will we know we can depend on God?

Lie #4: If I ignore my pain, it will go away. Our fear of criticism and scrutiny can lead us to suppress our feelings. Over time those feelings build, and they can end up spilling out, all over the people we care about most. We're so afraid to hurt or disappoint someone that we end up hurting and disappointing ourselves. It's a setup to become bitter.

The truth: If someone has hurt you or wronged you, God's Word is clear that you are to go and speak to your brother or sister in Christ and share your grievance with a loving spirit. Matthew 18:15-20 gives more insight about how to handle confrontation in Christ:

> If your brother sins against you, go and tell him his fault, between you and him alone. If he listens to you, you have gained your brother. But if he does not listen, take one or two others along with you, that every charge may be established by the evidence of two or three witnesses. If he refuses to listen to them, tell it to the church. And if he refuses to listen even to the church, let him be to you as a Gentile and a tax collector. Truly, I say to you, whatever you bind on earth shall be bound in heaven, and whatever you loose on earth shall be loosed in heaven. Again I say to you, if two of you agree on earth about anything they ask, it will be done for them by my Father in heaven. For where two or three are gathered in my name, there am I among them.

Expressing your feelings in a positive way and with the right heart can help you grow your relationships stronger. Each time you need to confront someone, face the timing and the situation with discernment. If you're confronting a nonbeliever, pray for wisdom on how to approach him or her. Maybe it is your supervisor or a coworker. Consider what you need to communicate and then do so in a loving way with a spirit of humility. The outcome most often will be a good one.

Confronting a friend can be difficult. Those closest to us know our secrets and our flaws, so we often avoid expressing our deepest feelings or comments about their actions because we don't want to seem hypocritical or judgmental. At the same time, we don't want our hurts to build up without a chance to have healing, especially when it is a dear friend. While some people may show their disappointment when they hear your feelings, it is important to seek an authentic relationship, which allows for honesty. Obviously each person and each situation is different; you'll have to discern whether or not it is something you truly need to verbally work out. If you're not able to talk directly to the person, share your thoughts with a counselor who can help you process your feelings so bitterness and anger don't settle into your heart.

You'll discover that when you approach people with a loving attitude, they are eager to reconcile or ease the situation. And you'll be surprised how many times a friend won't even know that her words or actions were hurting you.

Lie #5: Revealing who I am is a sign of weakness. Most of us have a fear of being vulnerable and opening up our hearts. Exposing our innermost thoughts and feelings puts us in a place of risk. We risk someone not reciprocating the feelings. We risk facing silence rather than affirmation. People spend a lot of time protecting their image for fear someone will think they're not as great as they are portraying themselves to be. Intimacy requires us to take off our masks and our public image. One of the most difficult things is to allow someone else to see the part of ourselves we have worked so hard to hide. Intimacy is built over time, very carefully, and with people we deem safe.

The truth: We are made for authentic relationships. The more real we are with people, the more we open our hearts, and the more freedom we'll experience connecting with others and with God. Fear of appearing weak is really inverted pride, and pride produces in us a puffed-up, protected spirit that no one is able to get through.

Lie #6: Everyone I get close to will eventually leave me. Many of us have been emotionally dropped at one point or another in our lives. Maybe it was a mother or father who abandoned us. Maybe a spouse left. Once we have experienced this type of abandonment, it's difficult to trust again, to love again, to have hope in another person again.

The truth: We must face the complete surrender of these relationships. When we form new relationships we have to release the people to God and just know that they are in our lives for a season or a lifetime. They are the Lord's, and so are we. God will never forsake us or leave us. In our darkest moment He will be here. When Job lost everything, it was God who revealed His faithfulness. Our hope, our trust, is not in people but in Christ. We are able to fully love God and know He will always be with us.

Lie #7: If I give things to God, my life will be out of control. Most of us want to be in control. We struggle with the fear of losing that control because we are afraid of the outcome. As I mentioned earlier, leaving the outcome to God is one of the greatest areas of overcoming. When we clench our little hands and refuse to allow God to work in our failures and our successes, we lose. I came to Christ when I had the revelation that I couldn't do things on my own. As much as I tried, I didn't have it all together. My knowledge and very limited wisdom hadn't worked for me. In fact, doing things my way had been detrimental.

The truth: If God created the heavens and the earth, and if we truly believe He is who He says He is, why wouldn't we believe He is big enough, smart enough, and kind enough to guide our lives? Can we rest in the fact that He does love us and only wants to give us the best in all things? He wants to give us godly, fabulous desires and then fulfill those in amazing ways. But past times of abandonment make us afraid to wish for, hope for, or believe—even in our God.

I heard a woman speak recently about writing down all her dreams, including her desire to work in an orphanage. She admitted that even as she wrote it down, she never thought it would be possible for her to live this dream. But God heard her, and a year later she was working in several orphanages around the world. When she shared her story, she could barely hold back the tears. She was amazed by her loving God who cared enough about her to give her the desires of her heart, once she gave her desires over to Him.

Now, get out the list of your fears I asked you to make earlier. Ask God to cover these specific areas of your life and to set you free. Take baby steps toward this freedom. You are actively involved in overcoming deadly emotions. You need to believe truth over lies and strength over timidity. Challenge yourself to face the fears you have. For example, if you are afraid of speaking before people, schedule an event where you speak before a few people on a subject you feel comfortable with. If you're afraid to confront someone when you feel you've been wronged, ask that person to lunch and share a thought you've written down so you can communicate everything on your heart (make sure this is done in love).

Keep your list handy. Write a godly truth next to every lie you have written down. Read through the Bible and find out what God says about fear...and your fears in particular. Here are a few truths to start with:

- God is with you (Isaiah 41:10).
- He will help you (Isaiah 41:13).
- He has redeemed you (Isaiah 43:1).
- Do not fear the reproach of man (Isaiah 51:7).
- Serve God without fear (Luke 1:74).

Deadly Consequences of Fear

Fear paralyzes. Fear was something I wanted freedom from, but I didn't know how to start. I remember sitting in the front row waiting to lead my first women's retreat. Fear had me in its clutches. Memories of past fears rushed through my mind. I remembered standing up to speak at a youth retreat and then running off the stage in the middle of my talk, crying and fearful. Now who in their right mind would humiliate herself again? Yet I knew that getting past the fear required that I get right back up there again. I had to answer the call of God on my life, and this meant more to me than the possibility of a humiliation revisited.

I'll never forget that night. I had been through the worst week. The kids and my husband had been sick, and I was exhausted emotionally and physically. I felt so weary and needed God to come through for me like never before. When the ministry leaders began to introduce me, I suddenly felt a cold chill come over me and my stomach went into knots. My mind drifted back to my many disastrous piano recitals as a child. My nervousness would cause my hands to sweat profusely and my little fingers would slip off the keys as I played. My piano teacher had high hopes for me to be a concert pianist, but my fear of playing in public never subsided, and those dreams died. Here I was, years later, and those same fears flooded my mind and sent my body into the same physical sensations of fear. I began to sweat and the familiarity of what had happened so many times before began to paralyze my thoughts.

I prayed, "Lord, help me! Speak through me, and give me strength and courage to overcome this fear." Right then I felt the Lord respond, "Do not fear, for I am with you." This is all God spoke to me. His voice was so clear that peace fell over me. As the ministry leader finished introducing me, I could feel my knees move my legs to a standing position but I don't remember walking up to the podium. The next thing I knew I was standing before the crowd, and I could feel the presence of God so strongly that peace permeated my entire being. From that moment on, I was assured that no matter who I had to speak to, no matter what assignment God would give me, He would never fail me and would always be with me.

This wasn't the last time fear would visit me, but it was the last time I allowed it to paralyze me and keep me from the promises God has for me. Every time those familiar physical and emotional sensations of fear arise and the enemy whispers to me a list of my failures, I resist believing it. I overcome this deadly emotion because I know my God is with me. I am not alone. He is whispering His truths to me so that I am not defined by past failures or the lies of the enemy.

Fear causes us to hide. We can easily hide behind a mask or an image of what we want people to see because we fear being found out. We tell ourselves, "If people really know me they won't like me." We're telling ourselves lies...and we're believing them! Hiding who you are is the same as telling God that He made a mistake in creating you. Standing behind a mask because it is more acceptable will not lead you in the direction of your purpose or gifts or contentment.

Fear can cause a heart to devise wicked plans. We can easily become afraid when we are trying to cover up sin or when we feel we are justified in revenge. Have you ever resorted to forming evil plans to get back at someone for a wrong he or she committed? What a slippery slope this is unless you have accountability in your life through friends, groups, church, and regular time spent in God's Word.

Fear can lead to lies. If we try to protect ourselves or our image after we have sinned or while we are sinning, we are allowing shame and pride to take over rather than trusting God with our situation or our healing.

Fear can cause us to become haughty. It is easy to become full of arrogance to cover up our insecurities. This is another way of self-protection, and it keeps us from experiencing the joy of intimate relationships—and sometimes keeps us from having relationships period.

Fear can cause us to run toward evil. We can become so afraid in life that we find solace or comfort in things that are spiritually, physically, and emotionally destructive. We run toward evil when we react with the world's answers and responses to situations that cause us to question God's role and His authority over us. If we are medicating with or turning to the world's solutions or to unhealthy solutions, we are turning away from the One who can help us.

Fear can definitely cause us to create discord. If we're not trusting of someone, we might elevate ourselves by planting seeds of division in order to keep control over that person or over entire situations. Fear and discord lead to jealousy and pride, as well as the sin of wanting to divide the body of Christ.

These are all deadly consequences of fear and the result of hiding sin. If we expose our sin and take it to the cross, we can reach up, surrender, and ask God to help us move forward unafraid and unashamed. We can't do this in our own strength. We need God to help us conquer fear. We need His Word to penetrate our hearts so we can step out in faith. When we take small steps to overcome fear in our lives, each step leads us to trust God and move away from the fear holding us in bondage. Eventually we are able to trust Him for all things, even when we don't understand or know the outcome.

Heart Bruises

I have a couple of friends who have such deep heart bruises that they are paralyzed in areas of their lives that God wants them to experience complete freedom in. They were both sexually abused as children. One of them hasn't walked the journey of healing and freedom. She can't face the pain and suffering that was such a significant part of her childhood. As a result, she has become very closed off emotionally. She is so afraid to face the past that she is unable to truly have a future. She was married, but the marriage ended in divorce. And she has no desire to have children because she fears she wouldn't be a good mother.

There are many lies this friend has chosen to believe that keep her imprisoned and unable to live life to its fullest. My heart is so broken for her, and I pray God will set her free. But unless she makes a choice to face her fears and heart bruises, she won't walk in the fullness of emotional freedom. Many dreams and desires remain unfulfilled in us because of this same resistance to surrendering our deadly emotions—and this is exactly where the enemy wants to keep us.

My other friend with a similar history of heart bruises has been able to face her fears and work through them over time. While abuse is a part of her past, it's not a part of her present. She has worked toward her healing and has moved on in her life. She doesn't allow her past to define her. She has a family and a healthy marriage and takes her pursuit for wholeness very seriously by seeking counseling when fears of her past revisit her present. She has experienced emotional freedom, spiritual growth, and deeper intimacy with Christ.

> Anyone who does not love does not know God, because God is love. In this the love of God was made manifest among us, that God sent his only Son into the world, so that we might live through him (1 John 4:8-9).

I have spoken to women in churches all over, and they've shared deep heart bruises that they are still trying to overcome. For all of us, this is a process. I've had to face my own past abuses, and it has taken years to get beyond some of the deeply imbedded fears and feelings of shame and guilt tied to those painful experiences. Some fears take more time to overcome, and it helps if someone can work through them with you...someone safe you can trust.

If you have faced abuses, my heart goes out to you. And I want you to know that emotional freedom is a lifetime journey for those who have these deep wounds, but freedom is yours to experience fully. While I believe most people require the assistance of counseling, my mother was able to work through the major emotional and physical abuses that she endured as a child by speaking and repeating the Word of God over her life daily and filling her heart and life with worship. Worship brings great healing, and God's Word has the power to change our lives in ways we never thought possible.

The Fruit of the Spirit Overcomes Fear

Fear is a feeling of apprehension, calamity, and dread. Experientially, fear is the feeling or sense that something unpleasant or even terrible is going to happen. God's Word adds more dimensions to our understanding of what fear is and a bit of a twist: "There is no fear in love, but perfect love casts out fear. For fear has to do with punishment, and whoever fears has not been perfected in love" (1 John 4:18). When we think in terms of opposites, we typically would pair love and hate as polar ends of the spectrum. However, if we consider this verse carefully, we understand that love is the opposite of fear. Fear cannot exist where perfect love does. How true this is, and what a revolutionary truth for those who seek balms and remedies other than God's perfect love to drive away the fears that lurk in their hearts.

Fear holds us in self-protection mode and keeps us running from love, intimacy, close friendships, and authentic relationships with everyone, including God. The word "perfect" used in 1 John 4:18 means "mature love." The more we trust in God's love, the more we grow and mature in our faith, and the less fear we have. Love is the fruit of the Spirit that drives out fear. Where perfect love exists, the fears that hold us in complete bondage cannot exist. Let's look at this fruit of the Spirit that helps us overcome the deadly emotion of fear.

Perfect love drives out fear. If we are growing in our relationships and learning to fully love God, ourselves, and others, fear becomes less and less a part of our lives. A wonderful result of this transformation is that love also leads us to the other fruit of the Spirit—joy, peace, and patience—that can help us stay clear of paralyzing fears. Do you feel joy? Peace? Are you patient with people around you? It is God's perfect will for us to be set free from the deadly emotions that try to overtake us. Rest in this promise: "For God gave us a spirit not of fear but of power and love and self-control" (2 Timothy 1:7).

Become a Life-Giver

None of us wants to stay in bondage to fear. It robs us of the freedom God so longs for us to have. I'm only able to give life to others in this area because I've been able to overcome fear by God's grace.

How many times have you told a friend about something exciting in your life, but because of her fears she says, "Are you sure you should do that?" "What if something happens to you as a result?" "What if you fail?" or "What if you get hurt?" These questions aren't based on godly wisdom; these types of comments are from people who are dream-robbers because of their own apprehension and cycles of fear. They rain on our parade and give us a long list of why we shouldn't step out in faith.

These are often the same friends or family members who will do whatever they can to steer away from anything that isn't a completely safe venture. I'm not just speaking of big things, such as a job, or a marriage, or having a baby. I'm speaking about small decisions, such as whether to fly on a plane, ride a bike to the store instead of driving, or going for a swim in a lake. I have learned to detect this tendency in some friends and family. I don't call them to report happenings in my life that I feel they are going to be negative about because of their fears. Are you the person controlled by fear? Do you offer affirming, encouraging words to others because you believe and have faith?

> So faith comes from hearing, and hearing through the word of Christ (Romans 10:17).

To stop the cycle of fear in our lives, to really be set free from it and embrace faith, we have to embrace God's truth. Notice how Paul indicates faith comes from *hearing* the Word of God. He doesn't say it comes from hearing positive words, but *hearing the Word of Christ.* We are always going to struggle with fear to some degree. I remember talking with Chuck Norris. When you think of the martial arts expert, you hardly think of a man who has fear. But he grew up with a lot of fear and had to learn how to not let it control him. In an interview I conducted for *Extraordinary Women* magazine, I asked Chuck about his fears and how he dealt with them. He reminded me faith was not the absence of fear, but simply the ability to overcome it, to face it head on, and to choose to trust God.

Just like in Connie's family, each of us has the ability to pass down fear. What do we want to give to our children, fear or faith? We have a choice to stop the cycle of fear that has been handed down through the generations. We can teach our children to overcome and to believe and have faith so they can go out and be life-givers in everything they do. Or we can become dream-robbers and rid them of their opportunities to fulfill their God-given purpose and step out in their destiny because of our unwarranted fears.

When we overcome fear, we're able to give love to others because we are no longer afraid of the outcome. We are no longer afraid to be rejected.

FREEDOM ACTIONS

Some fear, anxiety, and stress is normal, but when it gets out of control it impacts our lives on many different levels. Even our physical health can be threatened by manifestations of extreme worry: eating disorders, ulcers, headaches, migraines, and probably many illnesses. These deadly emotions can throw us so off balance that we become unable to function. Work becomes an overwhelming challenge, the kids seem out of control, and we definitely feel unsafe and out of control ourselves. The first priority needs to be our spiritual health. God is a God of order, and we are people who need that order to keep our emotional health at its best. I struggle with keeping this order in my life just like everyone else, but I find when I do, it keeps fear, stress, and anxiety away from me. Here are freedom actions for you to put into play.

1. *Take care of you.* I work hard to seek alone time with God. Because I look for times throughout my entire day, I usually have my Bible with me or a book I'm reading to help me in my spiritual journey. This time is essential. Talking with God helps to relieve our fears.

Spend time alone once in a while. Go to breakfast with a book or a journal, take a short trip to unwind, get a massage, walk in the mall, work out, or find hobbies that use your creativity and keep you feeling alive.

2. *Make "to do" and priority lists.* When I'm feeling overwhelmed or anxious, I make lists of things I need to do throughout my week. I also make a list of things that are on my mind and affect my personal life or my family's life. This helps get these concerns out of my head. Bringing order to your concerns and needs can help you feel more relaxed. And as you begin to check the items off the list, you'll find yourself becoming more peaceful and less fearful of what lies ahead. Take your lists with you in the car to write down ideas or things you need to remember to make good use of your time. Writing things down and coming up with a plan is a great way to relieve fear.

3. *Practice playful living.* While tending to our tremendous responsibilities, we can forget how to have fun or we adopt a mind-set that fun is for the young or those with little responsibility. But fun is for everyone and is especially needed for those who are weighed down with life issues. How much do you laugh? How often do you go to a movie, jump on a trampoline, watch the sunset, go for walks, listen to music, play games or sports, clap to music or dance (in the privacy of your home of course!)? Relieving the pressure that comes with greater responsibility is crucial to our vitality. I love to gather my kids in the living room and dance. We have dance contests and vote on who is the best that night. Make life an adventure most of the time around your house. Find ways to add excitement, spontaneity, and a spark of fun. For starters, play some great music and set the mood of joy.

4. *Learn to trust God and stay flexible.* This has been one of the greatest lessons I've learned—especially when it comes to my finances. I've had experiences with companies not paying me, people not

keeping their word, and other shifts that have caused my financial landscape to change. I've had to trust that God was in control. Relinquish your hold on your area of least flexibility. Maybe it's finances for you too. Or hospitality, generosity, work, commitment (or overcommitment), etc. Whatever area it is, practice going with the flow, keeping flexible, and waiting on God.

5. *Reflect on your fears.* Take inventory of your fears and ways that you stay fearful rather than faithful in trusting God. Spend time answering the following questions. Your answers will lead you to more freedom actions.

   • Are your fears irrational or real? What are some ways God has helped you overcome them?

   • What are the lies your fears tell you? What are the truths in God's Word that dispel those lies?

   • How has fear kept you from growing spiritually?

   • Was fear something you grew up with? If so, what are some of the lies your family believed that caused those fears? What would Jesus say about those fears? What are some ways you can break the cycle of fear? (For example, Connie's family was afraid of water, so she made sure her kids learned how to swim.)

   • What is keeping you from experiencing the fruit of the Spirit? List some changes you desire to make in your life that will help promote these—especially love.

   • Is fear robbing you of your dreams and your successes? What steps can you take to overcome in this area? Start with baby steps and gradually take bigger steps toward your goal. Spend time in prayer to be sure your dreams and desires are also God's purpose and plan for you. If you see God's favor and assurance in this area of your life, you'll feel confident to move forward.

- Next time you are tempted to say no when you're asked to try something new or outside your comfort zone, decide if your reaction is based in fear or caution. Caution is the result of wisdom and discernment; fear is the result of doubting self and God and hope. Act accordingly.

- Count how many times throughout the day you worry, and recite Scripture to replace your worry with trust and faith in God. Leave the outcome of your circumstances up to Him.

Freedom Prayer for Fear

Lord, You say in Your Word You have not given me a spirit of fear. I know this, and yet I'm still plagued with doubt and fear. Please heal my mind of these fears—transform my thoughts of fear to thoughts of faith. I'm not capable of overcoming fear with my own positive thinking or my own devices. Deliver me from fear so I can have peace in my life. Teach me what Your Word says about fear so I can have victory over my worries and anxious nature. Show me how to stay strong when fear threatens to overtake me. Help me make room for the presence of Your perfect love so there is no space for fear. Thank You for removing deadly fear from my life and restoring my thoughts to those of peaceful and joyful living. In Jesus' name. Amen.

He who dwells in the shelter
of the Most High
will abide in the shadow
of the Almighty.

PSALM 91:1

4

The Power of Jealousy

*If we would be angry and not sin (says one), we must be angry
at nothing but sin; and we should be more jealous for the glory
of God than for any interest or reputation of our own.*

MATTHEW HENRY

Keri struggled continuously with jealousy. She'd been betrayed in
several relationships with men and had also had a few friendships go sour. In each relationship she felt deceived and rejected. She
was now dating Alex and was very much in love, but she couldn't
shake her deep feelings of insecurity and the overwhelming fear he
would abandon her. In the relationship before Alex, she was married
to a man for several years who abused her physically and emotionally.
His desire for pornography and other women demeaned her for so long
her self-esteem was shattered.

Alex was not at all like Keri's former husband, but he had to deal
with the heart bruises caused by this other man. Every time he and
Keri went out, if he so much as spoke to another woman, Keri would
be gripped by anxiety and begin questioning him in a destructive way.
Keri's jealousy consumed her. She believed Alex cared for everyone
except her; she believed Alex really wasn't interested in her at all and
was with her only to pass the time. No matter how much Alex told
Keri he loved her, Keri couldn't believe it. On a spiritual and rational
level she knew it was healthy and good to give Alex a chance, but the
past, painful betrayals haunted her every time she took a step toward
trusting. She believed the feelings more than she was able to believe
God's leading and peace.

At the prompting of Alex, they began meeting with a counselor who would take her through the healing process of mending the pain of the past. Alex saw through Keri's out-of-control jealousy to her wonderful qualities and to her heart. He believed her heart could be mended. As Keri's healing progressed, she began to trust again, to feel a sense of hope in her and Alex's relationship. Keri would've torn apart her bond with Alex and with anyone else she met had she not gotten help and given her jealousy to God to be transformed into peace and hope.

Jealousy can destroy a company, a marriage, a family, a ministry, a friendship, and a life if it is allowed to. When jealousy is fleeting, it's more annoying than deadly, but this is the exact point where you need God's truth. If you dismiss a jealous thought because you know it's unfounded and a lie, the emotion has no power over you. But if you ponder the jealousy over and over, you will eventually act out your emotion and entertain it as truth.

Paul gives us insight into what to do with such thoughts: Cast them down when they exalt themselves against the knowledge of God. Bring the jealous thought captive to the obedience of Christ (2 Corinthians 10:5).

Has jealousy controlled you enough that it divided or devoured a relationship? Did the emotion become so powerful you couldn't see beyond it to act out of obedience to God? What does being obedient in this area of our lives look like?

The Root of Jealousy

Most of us are personally acquainted with jealousy. By definition, jealousy is "a lack of tolerance for unfaithfulness or resentment toward someone's successes, achievements, advantages in life, or relationships." By experience, it is "a green-eyed monster that shows up, seemingly out of nowhere, and takes over the situation." When we want to be enthusiastically supportive of a friend who received a recent promotion, the bad-mannered monster wants to sulk and express itself with bitter or belittling words rather than offer congratulations. Even when not expressed in verbal terms, jealousy makes its presence known through our actions and most definitely through our lack of sincerity if we do manage to say congratulations, but only through clenched teeth and a forced smile.

Jealousy denotes a feeling of resentment that another person has gained something we more rightfully deserve. Where does jealousy come from? Sometimes it's born of feelings of injustice. We feel we weren't dealt a fair hand. Someone else was given an unfair advantage over us. Why do we feel cheated?

At the root of the emotion jealousy is fear that someone is going to betray us, to let us down. We are afraid they won't meet our expectations and will fail to consider us. We are afraid they will abandon us or choose someone over us. But why are we afraid?

> But if you have bitter jealousy and selfish ambition in your hearts, do not boast and be false to the truth. This is not the wisdom that comes down from above, but is earthly, unspiritual, demonic. For where jealousy and selfish ambition exist, there will be disorder and every vile practice. But the wisdom from above is first pure, then peaceable, gentle, open to reason, full of mercy and good fruits, impartial and sincere (James 3:14-17).

Comparison Shopping

Jealousy can bring with it a very strange sense of losing a battle. A sense of "they won, I lost" comes over us—as if we're competing. And maybe sometimes we are competing for some kind of prize or job, but more often than not the sense of competition is based on our personal feelings of injustice and neglect or on a strong sense that we deserve more than we have or more than others have. Both scenarios present hearts focused more on others and ourselves than on God's view of us. And this unwarranted and inexplicable competition is so strong that it can rise up even between the best of friends.

One thing most of us do is "comparison shop." When we walk

into a room, we spend the first few minutes comparing ourselves to everyone in the room. We pan the room, either noticing all the flaws or what characteristics make the people superior to us. By the time we're through, we either feel great about ourselves or we feel jealous and horrible because we've decided that someone, if not everyone, in the room is better than us.

If you're a comparison shopper, your mood likely soars and plummets depending on your success, your looks, your material possessions. The truth is that someone is always going to look better, feel better, smell better, cook better, drive a better car, have a nicer house, keep up with her house better, and the list goes on. Yet we still struggle with comparing ourselves to others...even spiritually. Thinking things such as *If only I could be more spiritual like Susan* or *If only I had gifts like her then I could do more for God.* Do similar thoughts race through your mind?

All of us are capable of reducing people down to nothing, belittling them in our minds so we can feel better about ourselves. But it's exhausting to constantly be comparing ourselves to others, feeling like we're always falling short of God's expectations or those of our families or our bosses. In order to keep ourselves from this we must see ourselves as God sees us and not be afraid to accept truth.

Sometimes truth can be painful. We need to remind ourselves that God has His best in mind for us and will orchestrate His purposes even if we lose a husband to a lover, or a job to a coworker, or a best friend to another. God is still on the throne, and He is in love with us. His love never fails! If we accept our disappointments, our unmet expectations, and walk in grace as opposed to jealousy and resentment, we will become greater people.

Maybe you're the one hurting someone else because jealousy burns within you. If this is the case, work against your feelings by asking God to give you strength. Reach out to that person in love. Deliberately go out of your way to do things for her. What you will find is the jealousy will subside. Maybe not right away, maybe not even really soon, but eventually. Jealousy is a powerful, real emotion that is broken when you choose to love instead. Someone is the victim of your jealousy, but you and only you can choose to turn things around and make them a *recipient* of your love.

Finding Our Value

Jealousy was a continuous struggle for me throughout much of my life. Because of the shame and guilt I carried from my past, I didn't see myself as valuable. I interpreted anyone else's success as a comment on my unworthiness. The fear I had of abandonment and betrayal, much like Keri's, had formed deep insecurities in me. But as I turned my focus to who I am in Christ based on His Word, I was able to clear my negative thoughts and emotional patterns. My value—and your value—is not based on performance, material possessions, relationships, financial status, or anything or anyone. It's only based on Christ. We are children of God! We have no reason to be insecure or feel we aren't worthy of someone's love and affection. Embracing our value as God's creation is our power over jealousy.

I remember when I knew God was calling me to start a magazine. I kept asking God, "Lord, are you sure you have the right person?" I even came up with a list of names for Him that would do a much better job than I. He didn't buy it, and before I knew it I was launching a magazine.

If we base our self-worth on whether we measure up to other people, comparing ourselves to others with a critical eye, discounting others to lift ourselves up on a platform of perfection, we will never be at peace. There will always be someone out there to throw us off balance, to make us feel bad about ourselves. Jealousy is an act of desperation. What we initially believe is a way to protect who we are is really a trap of insecurity that keeps us from experiencing loving relationships—including one with God. Instead of drawing people to us, we push people away. They can sense our jealousy and envy. They can sense we can't handle being around them for whatever reason, and therefore we can't take joy in knowing them.

"The last will be first, and the first last" (Matthew 20:16), and yet so many of us are striving to be noticed, to be seen, to find our value. Where does our real value come from? Where does favor come from? If God lifts us up, if He will exalt us, then no one on this earth can take us down.

> We are afflicted in every way, but not crushed; perplexed, but not driven to despair; persecuted, but not forsaken; struck down, but not destroyed (2 Corinthians 4:8-9).

The Jealousy Factor

Why are we jealous? Why do we feel envious of others and what they have? What is at the core root of our jealousy? Here are some things you'll want to look at when thinking about your life and considering whether jealousy controls you.

1. Do you feel out of control often?
2. Do you feel anxious and fearful?
3. Do you feel insecure and compare yourself to others?
4. How do you see yourself?
5. How would you describe yourself?
6. Do you believe you are valuable?
7. Do you have irrational thoughts about others?
8. Do you smother people in your life?
9. Do you have difficulty trusting anyone?
10. Do you have obsessive behavior?
11. Are you overly possessive of things or people?
12. What is your greatest fear regarding being jealous?
13. Do you believe God loves you enough to never leave you or forsake you?
14. Do you love yourself and see yourself how God sees you?

Do your answers indicate you are sometimes out of control, fearful, anxious, lacking in belief that you have value and purpose, unable to see yourself as God does? Once you recognize this area of need in your life, your journey to freedom has an action step.

Why does God care if we are jealous or not? Why would it matter if we are walking in the flesh in this area of our lives? God, in His graciousness, cares so much for us He communicated clearly areas in our lives that would cause us to ultimately be destroyed if acted out. Sounds extreme doesn't it? And yet we see it quite often in the headlines of our daily news or even closer to home in our ladies' groups or weekly Bible study. All sin begins as a small seed, and when it is full grown brings forth destruction. What might be a little jealousy right now, if not dealt with, could become a full-blown issue that is eventually acted out.

God's Truth for the Lies of Jealousy

Jealousy becomes dangerous and destructive when we allow it to stir up inside us and then act on it. Just like all other emotions, jealousy begins as a thought. It moves to the heart, and then births feelings of fear, anger, envy, and division. When these feelings are evoked, what we do with them can be deadly poison. What are some of the lies we believe, and what does God's Word say regarding them?

Lie #1: We are not worthy or loved.
The truth: God truly loves us, and because of God's love for us, we are worthy and worthwhile. He loved us so much He gave His one and only Son, Jesus, as a living sacrifice for our sin and our shame, in order that we be free and made worthy (John 3:16). God loves us with an everlasting love (Jeremiah 31:3).

Lie #2: We can never measure up. Everyone else is better than us.
The truth: In our weakness Christ is made strong. He is glorified in our lives through our shortcomings because He is able to be our strength in those areas of our lives where we feel we are just not enough—not good enough, not pretty enough, and not smart enough.

We are sons and daughters of the King of kings, and this is not a small thing! Because we are His, we can depend on Him for our strength, for our wisdom, for our life. We exchange our life for His life, and our heart for His heart, and walk on the promises He has given us in His Word. This alone is where our value lies. We don't have to measure up to worldly standards or compare ourselves to others. We are not in competition with others because we have the peace of knowing that whatever we need God is enough. We are made perfect through Christ who strengthens us! "My grace is sufficient for you, for my power is made perfect in weakness" (2 Corinthians 12:9).

Lie #3: I can't go through another betrayal.

The truth: I remember saying this to my counselor. He replied, "Yes, Michelle, you can." No one wants to go through the pain of being betrayed or deceived, but we have to risk this if we are going to receive and give love. Loving involves risk; opening our hearts to intimate relationships involves risks. There are no guarantees in friendship or love or even in family relationships. But there are many guarantees that are ours to rest in as believers in Christ. God will never forsake us or abandon us! What we need to focus on is not whether someone will betray us or leave us, but rather, "Am I spiritually where I need to be so I can count on God to sustain me?" "If God is for us, who can be against us?" (Romans 8:31).

Lie #4: Jealousy will always control me. I can never be set free.

The truth: This, friend, is the greatest lie the enemy wants us to believe. As long as he can keep us convinced we can never overcome this deadly behavior in our lives, we will remain in bondage. Never be free? Ha! We *can* be free. God's Word tells us so! "For freedom Christ has set us free; stand firm therefore, and do not submit again to a yoke of slavery" (Galatians 5:1).

Jealousy Leads to Murder

When Cain brought his offering to the Lord, I'm sure thoughts of jealousy or anger weren't running through his mind. It wasn't until the Lord expressed pleasure over the offering of Abel, Cain's brother, and displeasure over Cain's offering, that jealousy reared its ugly head. Cain didn't follow the instructions God had given to him about his offering. He felt his way, his idea, was better than God's desire. God wasn't favoring Abel; He was simply pleased with Abel's obedience. When God saw Cain's anger, He told Cain how simple it would be to please Him. He revealed to Cain exactly what he needed to do: "Why are you angry...? If you do well, will you not be accepted?" (Genesis 4:6). Yet once again Cain's stubbornness and rebellious heart ignored God's instruction. He refused to repent and humble himself, and his anger burned even hotter inside his heart.

How many times have we ignored God's prompting because of our desire to hang on to a deadly emotion? Cain's anger and jealousy overtook him. He didn't let go of his anger, or his jealousy, and he killed his brother. He allowed his mind and his thought life to be consumed with lies, and these lies led to him murdering Abel. Where did Cain's thinking go wrong? What brought him to the place where his feelings became actions that would lead to the loss of his brother? *Cain probably believed:*

1. God loved his brother more than him.
2. Abel was better than he was.
3. Abel was trying to show him up.
4. He could never please God or be good enough for God.

The truth: God loved Cain *and* Abel. He gave them both the same tools to succeed. Abel put his heart into the choice of sacrifice because he loved God not so he could show up Cain. And God gave Cain another chance to succeed and encouraged him to not allow sin to overcome him. Cain could have pleased God so easily, but instead he let jealousy blind him.

What are the lies you believe as a result of jealousy? What does God's Word say about those lies?

The Consequences of Jealousy

Many crimes have been committed through the centuries due to jealousy and the lies people believe because of jealousy's nature that blinds us from truth. We hear about these things on the news every day, and in some cases we hear about them in the lives of our friends. If the enemy can keep us in a place of insecurity, of not recognizing our value, he can use this deadly emotion against us. Jealousy in its worst form eats at us and corrupts our beliefs regarding the very core of who we are. Two deadly sins that emerge from jealousy are 1) developing a heart to devise wicked plans and 2) becoming a false witness who breathes out lies (a gossip).

Jealousy propels us to turn dark thoughts into action. Out of insecurity and pain we try to gain a superior position over someone with the lies or negative things we say about them or with what we are communicating with our body language. We may keep these edgy emotions in check verbally, but our body language likely communicates exactly how we feel. That is why God has to deal with our hearts. We can have the truth about jealousy down pat in our minds and not have the truth in our hearts. And if we don't receive the truth with our hearts through the power of the Holy Spirit, we don't let it change our lives. The deadly consequences of jealousy include:

- destruction of relationships
- unmerited outbursts
- lack of contentment
- lack of peace
- obsessive behavior
- negative attitude
- torturous thoughts
- anxiety
- stress
- physical health problems

- anger
- insecurity
- shame
- paranoia

All of these can lead to destruction in the lives of those we love most and even innocent people who cross our paths. How many of us grew up with someone talking critically and negatively to us? The consequences were debilitating to us, and some people never get over the poisonous impact of someone's words.

Do we want to be bearers of these kinds of consequences in someone's life? How many times have you rained on someone's parade? They come to you excited about sharing something wonderful that has happened and, because you are jealous or envious, you act like it is no big deal, like it doesn't matter, or show no enthusiasm at all.

Are you dealing with deadly consequences yourself? When trying to determine if you are giving in to jealousy, ask yourself, "Does a threat truly exist to the purposes and will of God?" When you are battling insecurity, another person's achievements may come across as a threat. For example, a coworker gets a raise for putting in extra hours on an important project. Instead of being happy for her, you feel jealous even though you didn't put the same hours in. You interpret her promotion or favor from the boss as a personal reflection on your inadequacies. What you sow you may reap financially, physically, emotionally, and spiritually. Being focused on self-serving agendas and self-gain reaps destruction.

Some consequences of jealousy that keep you from being a life-giver are:

- not wanting others to succeed
- not wanting to encourage and lift up others
- having a critical spirit—putting others down to make you look better

- using negative talk—gossiping
- planning divisive plots—working against authority to create division

Remember what God's Word says about jealousy and selfish ambition: "Where jealousy and selfish ambition exist, there will be disorder and every vile practice" (James 3:16). When you feel yourself acting out in jealousy, ask yourself, "Why do I feel jealous? What is at the core of my jealousy? If my value is in Christ, and I trust Him with the outcome of my life, why am I jealous?"

The Fruit of the Spirit Overcomes Jealousy

Unfortunately, I don't think the fruit of the Spirit will ever make headlines, do you? However, if we embrace them as God's power against deadly emotions, we will have an easier time overcoming jealousy. We know engaging in jealous behavior is wrong. Yet jealousy can still surface, encouraging regrettable and shameful actions. What does this do to the person who is on the receiving end of our jealous behavior? And if they never know we are jealous, what does this do to us, to our hearts, to our relationship with God? What is the fruit of the Spirit that covers jealousy? Faithfulness!

Faithful brings to mind words such as "loyal, allegiance, devoted, dependable, accurate, true, dutiful, conscientious, and dedicated." Jesus called us to Himself, but He also called us to love others as ourselves, to treat others in a way we want to be treated (Luke 6:31). This love calls for faithfulness, and trust is one of the greatest qualities a faithful friend can have.

Jealousy is the opposite of trust. It is a complete lack of trust in others *and* in God *and* in ourselves. Jealousy deceives us by saying we aren't valuable enough for someone to be faithful to. If we don't think we are valuable, what are we saying about God? Why would a valuable God create something invaluable? We can offer faithfulness to others because our hope and our trust is in Christ. Nothing can harm us, hurt us, and destroy us, even if we were to die because our lives are in His loving hands. We are hidden in Him.

> He made my mouth like a sharp sword; in the shadow of his
> hand he hid me; he made me a polished arrow; in his quiver
> he hid me away (Isaiah 49:2).

When we begin to entrust the outcome of our lives to God—including the betrayal, the things worst imagined, the humiliation, and disappointments—when we begin to trust that we didn't get the new job because God had something better, we didn't end up married to someone we truly loved because His plan is greater, we release people and ourselves from the bondage of our jealousy, and we can embrace faithfulness as a foundation for living.

> No temptation has overtaken you that is not common to man.
> God is faithful, and he will not let you be tempted beyond
> your ability, but with the temptation he will also provide the
> way of escape, that you may be able to endure it. Therefore,
> my beloved, flee from idolatry (1 Corinthians 10:13-14).

Become a Life-Giver

> Having purified your souls by your obedience to the truth
> for a sincere brotherly love, love one another earnestly from
> a pure heart (1 Peter 1:22).

When a situation triggers jealousy in us, we must think of the big picture and consider who our jealousy will impact. What will be the outcome of any actions that are born of those feelings? This pause before our emotions can build gives us an opportunity to *choose a godly way* through the situation. It gives us time to choose a life of faithfulness.

Let's make decisions that bring life instead of destruction. If someone gets a job we want, if a parent seems to favor a sibling over us, if we lose a friend to another—whatever the case may be, God sees. He sees all, and He knows all, and we can leave the results of what happens in our lives up to Him and trust that He will work on our behalf. Scripture says, "Whatever you do, do it heartily, as to the Lord" (Colossians 3:23 NKJV). This leaves the results up to God. When we do this, it's not about pleasing someone else or performing for someone else; it's about pleasing God and becoming a life-giving person to others.

Here are five things you can do to encourage your new life-giving ways and resist the temptation to feel jealous:

1. Excuse yourself when others talk derogatorily about someone.

2. Confront gently when you are faced with gossip and jealous talk. For example, simply say, "I don't feel comfortable discussing someone else." This is not accusatory and keeps things peaceful, yet it does leave the other person to think on what she may have done to lead you to respond this way.

3. When you begin to compare yourself to others, quickly dismiss those thoughts and remember who you are—a daughter of the King of kings, a life-giving woman, a woman of purpose, someone made for greatness in God's kingdom.

4. Put others before yourself. Don't feel threatened by other people's victories and successes. Give when you don't feel like giving; love when you don't feel like loving.

5. Resist the idea of jealousy when it comes to your mind. Dismiss those thoughts and pray for strength to feel accepted and loved.

God demonstrates His protective jealousy of us in similar ways. Our hearts are in covenant with Him and Him alone. He is consumed with zeal to bring each person into a fresh and vibrant relationship with Him. His protective jealousy is a beautiful comfort to us and can bring us incredible security and sense of safety. His jealousy over us is a healthy jealousy and brings forth greater relationship between us and Him.

Jealousy Surrendered

I have watched my friend Bella time and again demonstrate an amazing depth of grace. I have listened to her give advice to women whose marriages or lives haven't turned out the way they planned. As she shares the wisdom that has come from personal experience, she does so with great compassion and strength. Whenever I meet a woman I admire, I know there is a story behind her strength, and Bella is no exception. As she shared her story, I knew I was hearing how God's grace replaces jealousy once it is surrendered.

Paul, Bella's husband, is a very talented music producer. On a particular project, he and a female recording artist named Cindy spent many hours collaborating. Night after night Bella waited for Paul to come home knowing he was at the studio with Cindy. When Bella expressed concern, Paul made it clear that he had no feelings for Cindy and was faithful to her. But still Bella felt jealousy rise up.

Bella could either believe her husband was being faithful or she could entertain long thoughts of Paul and Cindy laughing and flirting with one another. At first Bella didn't allow the jealous thoughts to rest in her mind. She believed the best of Paul. But as Cindy's career blossomed, the days and nights she and Paul worked together became even longer. Bella's mind wouldn't let go of the jealous thoughts anymore. Soon they consumed her heart and were manifested into actions. Bella screamed at Paul, cursing him in her torment. She even considered leaving him. Paul always assured her that his love and affection were only for her, but this wasn't enough. The situation peaked after Cindy went through a horrible divorce and then came to Bella to confess her love for Paul and her struggle with those feelings.

Now, come on...who could handle this without qualms? Seriously, most of us would go bananas if another woman came and said she was in love with our husband, especially if the woman was newly divorced. But Bella chose a different response.

She had met with her pastor and he'd asked her, "What is the worst fear you have in this situation?" She replied, "Paul would love her and leave me." And his response was, "And what would happen if he did?" Bella replied, "I would have to trust Christ and believe God would restore to me what I lost." "Exactly," was the pastor's response. "So release your feelings to Him and trust that Jesus will never leave you even if Paul does. If Paul chooses to walk away, you will be okay."

Bella had an epiphany. She walked out of the pastor's office and made a decision to trust Paul to the Lord and to fight for her marriage. She worked through her jealousy, her anger, and she released them to the Lord, knowing that even if the worst occurred, He would be there for her. Paul did not walk away. He never loved Cindy and was faithful to Bella. Cindy went on to remarry, and she and Paul lost touch. Paul and Bella held tightly to the bond and covenant of marriage. This is a beautiful picture of Christ's love. Bella and Paul have been married for more than 30 years now and have four beautiful children. If Bella's jealousy had controlled her and her actions, she wouldn't have reaped the beautiful rewards of a strong marriage. Paul and Bella wouldn't be able to minister to other couples by sharing their experiences. Their joy is a result of Bella's decision to surrender jealousy and leave the outcome to God.

We want to control a situation because we are afraid. This is where surrender becomes vital. We have to surrender every outcome to God and trust that even if our worst nightmares are realized, we will persevere with His help. Life is not easy and marriage is not easy. But with Christ we are never facing situations alone. And even if Bella had ended up without Paul, Jesus would still be with her, helping her to walk out her life. He never leaves us or forsakes us.

Bella could have destroyed her marriage and her children's future, but she chose to believe. She chose to walk in the Spirit rather than the flesh.

> So I say, live by the Spirit, and you will not gratify the desires of the sinful nature. For the sinful nature desires what is contrary to the Spirit, and the Spirit what is contrary to the sinful nature. They are in conflict with each other, so that you do not do what you want. But if you are led by the Spirit, you are not under law. The acts of the sinful nature are obvious: sexual immorality, impurity and debauchery; idolatry and witchcraft; hatred, discord, jealousy, fits of rage,

selfish ambition, dissensions, factions and envy; drunken-
ness, orgies, and the like. I warn you, as I did before, that
those who live like this will not inherit the kingdom of God
(Galatians 5:16-21 NIV).

FREEDOM ACTIONS

How do you deal with jealousy, the desire to self-protect, to guard
against someone taking something from you, or the fear of someone
doing injustice to you? What was God's desire for Cain? God said,
"If you love me, you will keep my commandments" (John 14:15).
Cain's jealousy overrode his desire to love and obey God, and he took
matters into his own hands. When you are tempted to take over your
life situation rather than submit a deadly emotion to God, consider
these truths:

1. *Believe God's plan and purpose for your life.* Scripture says it is God
   who works and wills to have His good pleasure in our lives. We
   don't have to strive in our own flesh or take matters into our own
   hands.

2. *Trust God's best for you.* The psalmist says if we delight ourselves
   in the Lord, He will give us the desires of our hearts (Psalm 37:4).
   God knows what's best for us. When we feel cheated or like we've
   been wronged or an injustice has been done to us, we need to trust
   Him and know He is here for us.

3. *Walk in the Spirit.* When you walk forward in the Spirit and deny
   the works of the flesh, you will savor freedom as never before. One
   of the works of the flesh is jealousy, and you must deny this in
   yourself. When you have a jealous thought, you can automatically
   know it is not of God. In practical terms, I do this by surrendering
   this feeling to God immediately. I refuse to allow these feelings
   to overtake me, and I choose to live and walk in the fruit of the
   Spirit: love, joy, peace, patience, kindness, goodness, faithfulness,

gentleness, self-control (Galatians 5:22-23). By doing this I am taking my thoughts captive and saying, "Lord, I trust You with my life and with the things and people that mean so much to me. I trust You with all things."

4. *Consider who you are jealous of and why.* Take inventory of such things to get to the heart of your emotions. Give these specific jealousies over to God so He can help you turn away the lies and usher you into truth and peace.

5. *Write a list and get creative.* Write out a list of who you are jealous of and then think of some acts of kindness you can do for them. This will help you overcome jealousy. It will also help you separate the deadly emotion of jealousy from your interactions with these people. You'll be amazed how your perspective will change.

6. *Actively pursue freedom from jealousy.* What are the barriers Satan uses to keep you in bondage to jealousy? What barriers do you erect to keep this deadly emotion in charge of your life? Write these down and then ask God to help you break through in these areas. Tell Him your desire is to be set free from the sin of jealousy and other sins associated with this negative stronghold.

7. *Tend to your heart bruises.* Which deep wounds in your life could be the root of why you are jealous? Write down what Jesus says to you about those hurtful places and what God's Word says about who you are.

8. *Know your true enemy.* Are people really out to take things from you, destroy you, or steal from you? Or is there an enemy who has come to steal, kill, and destroy? How has the enemy deceived you?

9. *No more comparison shopping.* Accept who you are in Christ, and look for ways to serve Him and fulfill His purpose for you.

Freedom Prayer for Jealousy

Lord, set me free from this deadly emotion controlling my life—from jealousy. Please forgive me for the ways I have let jealous behavior control me. Forgive me for not trusting You with the people in my life, the relationships in my life, and for the outcome of my life. Lord, help me overcome jealous feelings when they overtake me. Show me how to recognize them quickly and resist the temptation to entertain the thoughts that result in jealousy. Help me to take these thoughts captive and to remember the truth in Your Word so I won't be deceived. Thank You, Lord, for being with me and giving me Your strength to conquer this horrible deadly emotion in my life. Heal me and help me to not be afraid or feel threatened. And help the people who have been negatively impacted by my actions. Fill me with Your peace, Your love, and Your wisdom. In Jesus' name. Amen.

Your faith should not be in the wisdom of men but in the power of God.

1 CORINTHIANS 2:5 NKJV

5

The Deception of Lust

The soul, like the body, lives by what it feeds on.

JOSIAH GILBERT HOLLAND

When we experience heart bruises, we're often wounded emotionally, and from this pain we might make decisions, choices, and detours in life that we wouldn't have made otherwise. Lust might seem different from some of the other deadly emotions because lust itself can trigger other emotions, such as shame, jealousy, and even anger. But lust is like the other deadly emotions in that it doesn't emerge out of nowhere. If you examine the life of a person struggling with lust, you'll uncover heart bruises that helped shape, encourage, or give root to this deadly emotion. And like the other emotions we're facing together, lust is based on lies and deception that beget new lies and deceptions unless we overcome it with the power of God's Word, God's promises, and the strength of self-control made possible by God's intervention.

According to author and expert Dr. Catherine Hart Weber, the old saying "Hurting people hurt others" is very true. She and I had a conversation about this very thing, and she had a lot to share:

> We do repeat behavior because our wounds become a part of our emotional memory bank. It's what we've learned, and repeating what was done to us becomes a way of reacting to situations. A lot of times we do unto others as it has been done unto us. In most cases it's more than just misplaced longing. We somehow believe we can get those longings met through primary physiological passion, whether it is sex, or

food, or shopping. It is a conditioning in the pleasure center
in the brain. It's a very powerful thing. The brain becomes
conditioned to believe that you will receive pleasure from
the desire, and breaking the pattern takes the strength of
Christ in our lives. It has to become more than just self-will,
or discipline. We have strong wills, but this is so very powerful that it takes Someone greater than ourselves to help us
break free.

We misinterpret the temporary fulfillment we receive from
the forbidden passion for soul satisfaction. We have a longing
to be loved and our body and our brain crave to fill that place
of longing, so we find other ways of filling it. This could be
a result of being conditioned when we were younger. When
we ate food secretly, or discovered pornography, or engaged in
relationships with the opposite sex or same sex, it seemed temporarily satisfying. The problem with addiction is it never ever
really satisfies. It is empty. So we have to go back for more,
and that is how patterns of addiction and secretive behavior
and desperate behavior are established. It's a vicious cycle.

Dr. Weber went on to share with me what she has discovered while
counseling hundreds of women.

You have to get underneath and ask yourself what are your
primary needs: love, affirmation, fulfillment, meaning, and
acceptance, but sometimes it is just downright the lust of
the flesh. It feels good to overeat, to over-indulge. So what is
the solution? To move from the temporary satisfaction of the
cravings of the brain and body and fulfill the desires of the
Spirit and the deeper yearning of the soul. And we know that
the Son of God has come and has given us understanding
so that we may know Him who is true; and we are in Him
who is true, in His Son, Jesus Christ. He is the true God and
eternal life. Little children, keep yourselves from idols.

For those who have had bad experiences, like molestation or
abuse, they will struggle with confusing feelings, thinking,

"This is how I am satisfied," because their brains had a pleasurable experience in a twisted way. Somehow they have to now resist and recondition it. They have to live with the challenge of it and overcome with Christ.

Feeding ourselves through our carnal nature will time and time again lead us to emptiness and craving more of the same. Identifying what we are truly longing for is the key, and then meeting those needs in an authentic way. Stop and think, "Why am I doing this? Why am I moving from relationship to relationship? Why do I give my body away? Why do I overeat? What needs am I trying to meet?" Then begin to take the steps to move out of the addictive patterns and into spiritual wholeness. Take one step at a time and set goals toward moving out of the deadly behavior.

Again I saw all the oppressions that are done under the sun. And behold, the tears of the oppressed, and they had no one to comfort them! (Ecclesiastes 4:1).

The Root of Lust

Lust is any intense desire or craving for self-gratification. Unhealthy desires and the giving in to those desires is the root of lust. Whether it be lusting for material things, power, money, fame, someone else's possessions, a person, or sexual gratification, the root is based in selfishness and the feeding of our flesh. Whether it comes out of the pain in our lives or simply selfish desire, lust uncontrolled can be deadly. Hidden lust can go undetected by others, but God sees all our desires, and He longs for us to walk in purity of heart, not just in our actions before others. The lust we have in our hearts most often is never exposed unless acted out or admitted. We can confess our sins before God and be cleansed of unholy desire. Then He will strengthen us to walk a life of purity before Him. Our relationship with Him will keep us from the sin, not any rules we try to establish.

The Subtlety of Seduction

When we think of lust we tend to think of sexual sin, but lust is uncontrolled desire of any kind. As believers, lust takes the form of misplaced longings resulting in a life counterfeit to what God desires to give us. Deception is seldom direct. Seduction is subtle and usually undetected until too late. We can easily find ourselves in sin without ever intending to arrive there. When there is a weakness toward something, whether it is lust for food, a person, money, material things, at some point the enemy will tempt us in our areas of weakness and desire.

We may fight the battle of lust a while before we actually overcome the desire and no longer struggle. To grow beyond lust and conquer it we have to be sick and tired of the outcome, which is emptiness, loneliness, depression, shame, guilt, and unforgiveness, among others. Until we are tired of reaping these outcomes and ready and willing to fill ourselves with more of God, we won't change. God desires for us to have nothing greater in our hearts than Him. When we choose other things or people over God, our love is displaced and the flow of Christ's love doesn't easily move through us.

We can sometimes overlook material things and food, but when a person comes into our lives and tells us what we want to hear—what we long to hear and don't hear or haven't ever heard, and what we feel we need to hear—the longing and void in our lives can override our commitment to obedience. The yearning for connection with another person, whether it be emotional, spiritual, or physical, entices us and seduces us to the point we suddenly find ourselves in dangerous territory. Let's look at a few types of attractions we need to be cautious of.

Emotional Attraction

> Brothers [and sisters], if anyone is caught in any transgression, you who are spiritual should restore him in a spirit of gentleness. Keep watch on yourself, lest you too be tempted (Galatians 6:1).

A friend came to me for advice on how to handle an emotional attraction. She had moved to Los Angeles to pursue her lifelong dream of a film career. My friend and her husband had both agreed that she should take this chance, make the move, and they would carry on a long-distance relationship. Even the strongest marriages struggle in long-term, long-distance situations, and their marriage wasn't strong enough for this. They had been going separate ways for a long time, mainly due to their different pursuits. He was in a very successful business career, and she was focused on the beginnings of what could be a major acting career. The seduction of fulfillment from their careers was overriding their love for each other and their understanding of how to protect that love.

My friend was talking with me on this day because she realized she was developing an emotional attachment to a male actor who was playing her onscreen boyfriend in a film project. She had kept her distance at first, but she was lonely, far from home, and the desire to talk with someone, to connect with a male who was paying attention to her, outweighed her conviction. And it seemed the attraction was mutual. The two were together a lot, and the emotional tie was growing stronger. As she explained her situation, her face lit up when she mentioned his name. I could see he had found a place in her heart. I knew I had to be honest and direct.

Clearly the emotional attraction was leading to physical attraction. I knew it was only a matter of time before destruction would come. As only a friend can do, I told her she needed to cut it off and even quit the film if she had to. She was not strong enough to be away from her husband, and her marriage wasn't strong enough for this situation to continue. Her response was one of pleading: "Michelle, I can't. I can't shut this man out of my life. Couldn't we just be friends?" But this would just be another deception by the enemy. Her feelings were so heightened by this person and his affection and attention, the only way to avoid the problem was to put some distance between them. By coming to me and exposing her heart and her temptations, she was calling out for help.

If I had only spoken about shame or judgment to my friend, she might've given up her pursuit of godliness and the emotional attraction would've taken over her life.

Who is struggling around you? Are you judging them, or are you reaching out to them with compassion?

Physical Attraction

> Watch and pray that you may not enter into temptation. The spirit indeed is willing, but the flesh is weak (Matthew 26:41).

Being a victim of sexual abuse by a boy in high school and experiencing other heart bruises as a result, I know all too well how easy it is for heart bruises to play a part in forming addictions. Whether it be sexual addiction, relationship addiction, or alcohol addiction, we find ways to medicate our pain until we choose to take the healing path we need and pursue a journey of wholeness.

Lisa was sexually abused as a young child by several men. Two of the three men who abused her used pornography. If you met Lisa today you would never imagine those atrocities were part of her life. She looks like your typical "have it all together" kind of gal. She is very confident in the way she comes across and very attractive in the way she presents herself. Her demeanor is definitely not the look of a woman who has endured painful abuse. Lisa's journey has been one in pursuit of freedom, which has healed her brokenness. Here is her story in her own words.

> Lust became a part of my life at age three, but I never really held the three men accountable for what they'd done. In fact, I justified their sin by believing they had struggles with lust, and I was an innocent victim of their desires. It was later in life, when I became a believer, that I began to look at the serious reality of what had taken place in my life and how the abuse had impacted me physically, emotionally, and spiritually.
>
> As a result of the sexual abuse and the porn that was used, a very perverted picture was painted for me and a lie was communicated:

This is how all men view women. It also communicated a second lie—that women, like those I saw in the magazine, who use their bodies to have power over and get approval from men, are glamorous and strong. Sadly, [my situation] made me want to be one of those girls. Out of my abuse, I was taught the extreme perversion of God's plan for a loving healthy relationship. I was taught that if you want to get love from a man, you have to be an object of sexuality.

As I got older, I knew enough to know promiscuity was not right, but my view of love was so skewed that it caused me tremendous pain and sorrow for years. I struggled with strong sexual desires in every relationship. And honestly, I had a great sex life in those relationships. I didn't have any shame over my body. But what was missing was the beautiful depiction of what sexuality was meant to be in the covenant of marriage and the beauty and spirituality it brings if two people are in love with God and one another.

I understand now that I used my sexuality as a way to keep a man's interest in me. I believed the greatest lie: Love equals sex, and in order to have love I had to engage in sex. I went through a period in my early adult life where I became bitter at those who hurt me, and that bitterness toward men caused me to use men for sex. I wanted to use them before they used me. My sexuality was driven by the deadly emotion of lust, along with control and bitterness. And it wasn't just about sex, but it was about sensuality, about the way I dressed and the way I communicated. This drive to perform was exhausting.

Finally there came a turning point, and I heard the Spirit of God whisper into my heart that He wanted me to come home to Him. That day I broke down and repented and gave my heart to God in a way I had never done before. This began the journey of restoration in my life. I began to get into the Word and really focus on what God was saying to me personally.

After talking it over with a friend, I discovered that the root of my issues with lust was the exposure to pornography and the sexual abuse in my life. I didn't know how to relate to a man without the component of sex in there. This was the beginning of my journey to freedom. What I began to understand was that trying to control my behavior through shaming myself and abiding by rules was not addressing the root of the problem. I was controlled by my wounds, and they were winning.

My whole focus was not on the Lord, but instead it was completely on how to manage my desires and lust. My church at the time (and many other churches) had the bad habit of putting more shame and guilt on people who already felt tremendous shame and guilt as a result of their heart bruises. Unfortunately, we pile more shame and judgment on these wounded souls instead of saying, "Let me walk beside you in the areas of freedom you are pursuing," "Let me be here and be strength to you, and even if you end up falling, I will be here to walk with you as you gain strength." Jesus did this with people. This is why He was able to embrace Mary Magdalene, the prostitute, and the adulterous woman in Luke 7. He saw beyond the pain and into the heart of people, and with grace He extended His love to them and asked them to follow Him.

Now I am free. I know God is not this God sitting there waiting for us to make a mistake so He can "out" us to everyone. My God is here to help me, to love me, to free me. It is okay to live out the process. God has also shown me that I am worthy of more than lust from a man. I am worthy of being loved for the sweetness and richness of my soul.

Most of us hide lustful notions we have and keep them under control unless tempted, and then there is a choice to give in or to resist. Lisa's lustful struggles were the result of lies communicated to her through abuse when she was a child. She was basing her entire identity on these lies. What God had to do for freedom to come to Lisa was to reveal His truth. And she chose to follow that truth toward His acceptance and His unconditional mercy and love.

As I've ministered, I've had opportunity to hear many stories of people who are enslaved to sin or struggling with great temptations. I am reminded time and time again that without Jesus none of us is able to walk in the obedience and joy He so desires for us.

Spiritual Attraction

> And you will know the truth, and the truth will set you free
> (John 8:32).

Is there such a thing as spiritual attraction? Absolutely. And this could be the most seductive and dangerous of all lusts because it is so subtle. We've heard of affairs by people in the pulpit and we wonder, *How can this be? He is a pastor, a leader.* And yet one of the most subtle ways the enemy can get to us is when we are in relationships with other believers. Our guard is down and we are more open and vulnerable because the Holy Spirit is actively working in our lives.

Let's look at Pam's story. Pam had always guarded herself against anything that could lead to adultery, but at one point in life, she found herself going down a path led by her strong desire for spiritual intimacy. It started out innocently. Pam and a male coworker had become good friends. They had the same gifting so they often worked together on projects. During this time, they began to open up about their mutual heart for the Lord. They were both leaders in their respective churches and mature in their walks of faith. Eventually they began emailing one another regarding work. Over time their exchanges became more personal, exploring faith and life. They also shared with one another that their spouses were uninterested in talking about God. The more they shared with each other, the safer they felt and the more common ground they discovered.

Their emails were never sensual. Pam believed that because she included God in the conversation the exchanges were harmless. But the emails did become more personal. Her coworker would flatter Pam with beautiful emails about what an amazing woman of God she was and what a gift she had for her work. This praise filled a deep emotional and spiritual need in Pam, one that hadn't been fulfilled by her husband or others. Pam found herself looking forward to each email exchange. A strong bond formed, and still Pam felt it was harmless. Her husband knew of the friendship so she felt safe. But a dream revealed the danger of this lie.

In Pam's dream, she and her coworker walked hand-in-hand through a city. They came upon two beautiful high-rise buildings. As Pam looked up to admire them, the buildings began to fall apart. Pieces tumbled to the ground and rolled into the ocean to be swept away. When she awakened, she felt God was showing her how the buildings represented their two beautiful lives and futures and how those lives and futures would be destroyed if they continued the friendship.

The power of this dream and the unveiling of the truth left Pam sobbing. She cried out to God, asking Him not to require her to give up this friendship that felt like one of the greatest things that had happened to her. But she felt God revealed the bigger truth, that He was that in her life. He was the love, acceptance, support, and source of peace for her. He was the One ready to listen to her heart every time she wanted to communicate it.

She knew what she had to do. This coworker had become an idol, a replacement for her spiritual relationship with her husband and even a replacement for the peace she needed to find in God. When she told her coworker of the dream, they immediately cut off contact. They even avoided working together because the spiritual attraction presented them with the desire for more. Pam admits that what started out to be innocent had become deadly and consuming, and if she had not been warned, she believes it may have ended up in an affair.

Are you crossing boundaries in any of your relationships? Be wise and move away from these relationships and toward your spouse. If you are single, don't let these types of relationships lead you to a path of lust or unfaithfulness in your walk or in someone else's walk. Your actions could be leading someone else astray. Consider the ramifications, the consequences of every action and every exchange. Bring all of your relationships before the Lord.

An Affair, a Murder, an Unplanned Pregnancy

There are numerous examples of lust in the Bible, but one that leaps out is the story of King David and Bathsheba.

Bathsheba was bathing, and from the roof of his castle David laid eyes on her. He sent a servant to inquire of her and found she was the wife of Uriah. David disregarded her marriage to Uriah and called her to him. He slept with her while Uriah was away in battle as a member of David's army. Later, after finding out Bathsheba was pregnant with his child, David called a servant to retrieve Uriah from the battlefield. When Uriah returned, King David told him to go home and eat and sleep and be with his wife. David was hoping Uriah would sleep with Bathsheba so the consequences of adultery would be kept hidden and people would think Bathsheba's child was her husband's. Uriah, being a loyal warrior, refused to go home and be comfortable while his men were on the battlefield. He instead slept at the door of the king's house. Since Uriah didn't sleep with Bathsheba, David had to come up with a second plan to hide his sin. He ordered the army to retreat from Uriah on the battlefield so Bathsheba's husband would be unprotected and killed. This deadly deception went as planned. David waited for Bathsheba to mourn the loss of her husband and then took her as his wife. They had the child, but the Lord was angry with David and didn't allow the child to live.

King David's pursuit of Bathsheba was a devastatingly selfish act that caused the death of others and much suffering to many more. David later repented, and God blessed him with another son, but the consequences of his sin were still very great.

What We Lust After

Selfish desire and lust are all about us, placing value in "things" and "idols" rather than in God. And as Dr. Weber noted, sometimes it just feels good to take what we want. What we're lusting for becomes an idol, and just like the Israelites who worshiped other gods, or David who saw a beautiful woman and decided to bring her to his bed, we too are left in a heap of destruction when we choose something empty that yields dangerous consequences instead of what is alive and abundant—Jesus Christ and His principles.

Humans are creative beings who find many things to lust after. Let's look at a couple.

Lust for Power

I had a friend who worked for a megachurch, but the leaders eventually disappointed her. They appeared to be going down a road that was about fame, power, and money instead of the ministry they had been so passionate about in the beginning. My friend was an active part of building this mega empire, and she felt so deceived and disappointed in her participation in something that wasn't at the core, authentic. But what may have looked like rash and shocking decisions by the leadership were most likely the result of ideas long-harbored in their hearts. The lust for power and fame became greater than their love for God. Probably without even realizing it (remember the devil works through subtle seduction), they found themselves in a place far from what their original vision represented. Opportunity revealed their lust and met a deep need in them to have fame and power. They gave into those lusts and acted out in them.

How about you? Do you try to fill deep longings with things other than relationship with Christ?

> But you, O Lord, are a God merciful and gracious, slow
> to anger and abounding in steadfast love and faithfulness
> (Psalm 86:15).

Lust for Acceptance

Can acceptance become an idol in our lives? Absolutely! Some people will do whatever it takes to feel accepted. They'll sacrifice their morals, their integrity, their families just to be accepted by those they hold in high esteem. This is the case for Shane, whose deep longing led him to places he never thought he'd go. The first time I met Shane I was fascinated by his willingness to freely lay his life before others. He has a tremendous passion for Christ and walking in the obedience the Christian journey requires. After hearing his story I saw why he so vehemently clings to Christ not only as Savior, but also as his deliverer. Shane is a very handsome guy—sort of a combination of George Clooney and Clark Gable. You'd never know he struggled with self-worth most of his life. Shane's looks, personality, charm, and success didn't equate to the fulfillment, confidence, and acceptance he longed for. Those things of the world couldn't save him and love him. Only God was able to work that miracle. Here is his story:

> I grew up in a very performance-oriented, driven family. I am the seventh child born in a family of 8 kids and was born into a very affluent Catholic family. However, by the time I was 12 my dad lost all of his money. While my dad never sat down to discuss his expectations for any of us, the expectations were understood. I felt from the beginning that I couldn't meet his standard and was, therefore, unacceptable. Not only that, but I was so different from my siblings that I felt something was grossly wrong with me. Being creative and having what our culture considers "feminine" qualities made me different. The rejection I faced drove me to the lies of the enemy. One of the greatest deceptions was, I am so different, I must be homosexual.
>
> James Dobson painted the most beautiful picture in his book *Bringing Up Boys*. He describes how we were all made different. We are not all hands. We are all given different dispositions in life. So many men are convinced they were born this way, and the answer is yes, you were born sensitive, you were born to belong to the poets of this world, and we are the writers, the reflectors, the creative ones—but God did not make you homosexual.
>
> Dobson also discusses how a boy is looking for that imprint on his life from his father; how he is looking for that affirmation, that bond. Did my dad ever look at me and tell me that I mattered? No. That kind of outward love was not a part of his upbringing or his generation. I was a sensitive kid who needed touch and affirmation and a feeling of acceptance. So I spent most of my life trying to find the acceptance, the affirmation that I was craving.
>
> In my desperation to understand masculinity, my view became more perverted. I was in bondage while living the lifestyle many who are

not saved would envy. I was dancing with one of the greatest shows in the country and traveling to other countries with the cast. I was trained under the top choreographer in the business. I had money and was surrounded by beautiful people—and I was sleeping with most of them. Yet I was empty. I attained all the material wealth, the fame, and all that goes with it, but I could also see what those things yielded—loneliness. Even during my worldly success, I thought it was always an accident because at the core of my being I didn't feel worthy. I didn't feel accepted or loved.

My life started to change when a fellow dancer and choreographer told me she was a born-again Christian. I was appalled at the whole idea of Christianity because it immediately made me feel unaccepted. When I told her I was homosexual, I was sure she'd reject me immediately. Instead, she looked at me with such humility, such grace, and said, "Shane, God loves you! He may not like your sin, but He loves you and He can heal you!" As she spoke, I remember thinking to myself, *You are so full of crap. There is no way I can get out of this life I am in.*

Finally God got my attention. One night during a short break, I felt God telling me to ask my friend Susie about the Bible study she was going to. So I did, and she asked me to come along. Suddenly I found myself accepting her invitation. I walked out the back door to go home and it hit me, *What did I just do? I have got to get out of it.* During the rest of the week, I tried to think of ways to get out of it, but I couldn't tell her I wouldn't go. So I went. And after the Bible study the pastor asked if anyone wanted to give his or her life to the Lord. I knew in my heart I needed something, but my pride was keeping me from having to "look" like I needed something. So after his invitation, I half-kneeled and prayed. I was thinking, *I hope these people don't think this means anything to me.* But I'll never forget being overcome by the thought of those things that had artificially made me feel accepted contrasted with the sincere feelings I had as I asked Jesus to come into my heart. On that day, the photos in the magazine, the success, the money, the sex, and everything else—I offered them all up to God…every bit of them.

Thank God I was so naïve because had I known the cost I probably would have evaluated it more heavily and who knows where I'd be today. The pastor gave me a Bible, and I read it constantly in the days following. After the fourth day, I woke up in the middle of the night, and I knew in my heart for the first time ever that someone loved me.

This began one of the hardest journeys of my life because it was a process of renewing my mind and my spirit. It was a dying to the flesh and to my lustful desires and all I had lived for. The journey was more about my healing than about getting rid of my sin. Looking back, what I've learned more than anything is the quest is not just about the healing, but the quest must be Christ and all He is and stands for. There is no quick fix, there are no formulas. Every journey is different.

Christ's acceptance of us looks like "I love you because you are special; I love you just as you are in all your sin and junk." At first I associated God's love for me on whether I had sin in my life or not. I knew I couldn't overcome sin, and therefore I didn't believe God loved me. I didn't separate the sin from the sinner. Fear was at the root of what I was struggling with. The lies that "I am not worthy, I am not good enough, I am not accepted" were all at the root of the lust in my heart. How wonderful it is to recognize you are broken and have the opportunity to go to the cross and find completeness in Christ! The whole idea of "I need to get my act together" and the idea of "grace and mercy on the sinner" must coexist. We do need to walk in obedience to Christ. We do need to say yes and amen to the things of righteousness, and yet, when we or others around us sin, we also have to extend the mercy and grace God extends to us. If my friend had not extended God's grace and mercy, but just His desire for obedience and rules, I might not be a believer today.

God's Truth for the Lies of Lust

So what are some ways we can keep ourselves from believing lies the enemy feeds us when it comes to lusting? When we are in the midst of lust or such strong passionate desire, the emotion itself may seem overwhelming. We feel at the time that all we can do is gratify the craving that is consuming our thoughts and emotions. So how do we work against this? Here are four lies the enemy will try to feed you in the midst of your desire.

Lie #1: All of my feelings are real and true. When we are caught up in desire, we feel as if we can't live without what we are lusting for. As Dr. Weber said, the pleasure center in our brain is craving what we have learned to desire or what we have been feeding ourselves to satiate our desire. Basically, like an addiction, these longings override our logic, morals, and boundaries. If we continue to believe in our feelings even when they are telling us we "need" something more than we need God, we will remain in the bondage of our sin.

The truth: What we need is in the Word of God. His Word transforms our hearts and destroys the hold lust has over us and our thoughts and actions. What we need is God's truth to weigh against our feelings.

> For the desires of the flesh are against the Spirit, and the desires of the Spirit are against the flesh, for these are opposed to each other, to keep you from doing the things you want to do (Galatians 5:17).

Lie #2: If I hide it, I am safe. As long as we hide it, God can't begin the healing. When we refuse to share our fight with lust with someone, it is usually because we have found a way to rationalize it and keep it to ourselves. Self-deception is a big part of the addiction cycle. We want to believe that if we keep a sin from the eyes and awareness of others, then there is nothing wrong with what we're doing. But what most of us know, deep down in our hearts and spirits, is that once we've exposed our sin, we'll be required to deal with it.

As difficult and destructive as it is to live out deadly emotions and their consequences, there is an attraction and deception that is even harder to let go of. Healing sounds difficult, if not impossible. And we fear failing and letting down God and others in our lives.

The truth: Freedom comes when we expose our struggles to someone safe, someone grounded in God's Word and truth. Seek counseling and support as you need it. Never feel shame in seeking healing. God shapes miracles out of our mistakes. He is glorified in our weakness because His strength is revealed when we walk toward wholeness.

> I say, walk by the Spirit, and you will not gratify the desires
> of the flesh (Galatians 5:16).

Lie #3: If I pretend it didn't happen, it will go away. This sounds similar to the previous lie, but it is a little different. Some people not only don't speak about their sin, they actually tell themselves that nothing has happened. They stuff the experiences into the darkness and never look back. Unfortunately, the consequences are never buried for long. They reemerge in our behavior, our thoughts, our actions, and our spiritual walks. The deception that is planted at the time of our sinful actions and mistakes take root. Suppressing it only prolongs bondage.

The truth: The sin won't go away, but it can be forgiven. First, you must not ignore the sin, but you must sincerely repent of it. Once you've exposed it and have put truth (God's Word) up against it, get on your face before God and deal with it just like King David did. He repented and God restored. If you fall again, repent again, but instead of focusing on the sin, focus on going deeper with Christ. Focus on His acceptance of you, His mercy for you no matter how many times you mess up, and His grace that will help you resist the power of sin so you can change. Your relationship with Christ will eventually overcome the sinful desire. It will leave you, my friend. I can attest to this!

> And those who belong to Christ Jesus have crucified the flesh
> with its passions and desires (Galatians 5:24).

Lie #4: What I crave and what I desire will satisfy my deepest needs.
No object, no person, no relationship can ever satisfy you the way
God will satisfy you. You may feel a temporary satisfaction, but then
you're left with shame, guilt, and depression. Get to the root of your
desire. Remember your sinful behavior is about some kind of longing
and most likely is based on some insecurity, some lie you've embraced
along the way that says, "You're not good enough," "You're not pretty
or handsome enough," or "You're not acceptable." The lies say, "Without these lusts being gratified, you are not going to be fulfilled."

The truth: You are fulfilled through Christ and in Him alone.
Spend time talking through the lies you've believed about yourself or
the pride you've built up because you are trying to protect an image.
Expose your heart and the humanity of who you are. This will help
you overcome lies.

> For freedom Christ has set us free; stand firm therefore, and
> do not submit again to a yoke of slavery (Galatians 5:1).

What we do with strong, deadly emotions when they arise depends
on the tools we have to overcome that area of trial. Sometimes it can be
as simple as asking ourselves why we want something and questioning
whether we really need it. King David, whose whole existence as king
was due to God giving him wisdom to overcome a giant, couldn't
conquer the giant of lust when it came to him. Instead he gave in to
his lust. Bathsheba was someone else's wife, and his decision to take
her caused him to not only sin in lust, but eventually in murder. He
found himself so taken by her, that he had to have her at any cost.

Have you lusted after something of someone else's and demanded it
at any cost? Have you hurt people as a result? Have you hurt yourself?
A lot of pain and sorrow followed David after he sinned. Will your
lustful desires and actions cause you to hurt yourself and others? Will
it bless others, prosper you, protect others, and be a joy to others?

In truth, consequences alone don't keep us from going after the
lusts of our flesh, otherwise there would be less divorce, less adultery,
less addiction to pornography. So if consequences won't keep us from

sin, what will? We keep going back to one thing: our relationship with Christ. The deeper we go with God, the more we have relationship with our Savior, the more we have His heart for the things that are pure, holy, and of good report.

Deadly Consequences of Lust

> Speaking loud boasts of folly, they entice by sensual passions of the flesh those who are barely escaping from those who live in error. They promise them freedom, but they themselves are slaves of corruption. For whatever overcomes a person, to that he is enslaved (2 Peter 2:18-19).

Once lust moves from thought to deed, we become enslaved to our desires. When we are able to allow the "wind to just blow by us," we are able to overcome the control sin has on our lives. If we don't seek healing and strength, we will experience deadly consequences. Here are some consequences we'll experience with lust and other deadly emotions we give our hearts over to.

We're enslaved to sin. What happens when we, as believers, give in to sin? We are met with shame and guilt. If we don't repent but instead continue to walk in the sin, it continues to enslave us because we continue to believe the same lies about ourselves. There are two more lies we believe that will keep us in bondage.

We believe our identity is the sin. If Shane continued to live in this lie, he would still be living in the sin he was enslaved to. He had to see himself as loved and accepted by Christ in order to be set free. No one can prove this to you or force you to accept this. Acceptance only comes through understanding that forgiveness is a free gift from Christ, and we have to embrace it to receive it in our lives and be free from our pasts.

We begin to believe overcoming is impossible. The quest for our freedom is really the quest for Christ. The more we fill ourselves up with

Him, the less we want the sin. The more we fill ourselves up with His truth, the more we will believe we are forgiven. The objects of our lusts, such as pornography, adultery, incest, assault, abduction, sodomy, rape, money, and power, are destructive, but the acting out of our lusts eventually leaves us emotionally bankrupt.

It is easy for sin in our lives to go unrecognized, especially when we have rationalized the purpose behind it. What happens to our emotions when we continue to live in sin as believers? We find ourselves easily agitated, depressed, frustrated, ashamed, fearful, paranoid, and angry because when we live in sin we are going against the Holy Spirit in our lives. We are going against our consciences and against God. When we struggle with continuous sin and temptation, we start to believe it is impossible to get out of the cycle. This is why our quest must be for more of Christ and less of ourselves. We deny the things we are lusting for, turning away and refusing to accept the sin. Then we're on the road to freedom.

> O my God, I am ashamed and blush to lift my face to you,
> my God, for our iniquities have risen higher than our heads,
> and our guilt has mounted up to the heavens (Ezra 9:6).

This was the Israelites' response after marrying foreign women (which was forbidden) and breaking faith with God. Our response is the same when we break covenant with Him and go after the lusts in our hearts. We're chasing after our own desires instead of seeking God's perfect will for our lives that brings us to a place of peace and contentment.

The Fruit of the Spirit Overcomes Lust

What is at the core of our lust? Why do we long to fill ourselves with something other than God? Why are we choosing to worship idols? When we embrace the lusts of our flesh, we live and breathe sin as a result. We are choosing something else over God. We are choosing to worship sin rather than worship God and His righteousness. This comes from lies we believe, such as: God is not enough, we need the sin, we can't live without the temporary satisfaction the sin brings, or the sin will heal us. These are just a few of the lies we choose to believe over God's truths that He is enough, He is the only one who can truly fulfill us, and He is the healer, the lover of our souls. What we are choosing is a counterfeit to the real thing—Jesus Christ. The part of the fruit of the Spirit that overcomes lust is self-control.

God hasn't put anything before us that He hasn't given us the ability to overcome. Yes, we need Christ to strengthen us, but we must also exercise self-control. We must learn to not react to things we want and desire by taking what we think will gratify our desire. Instead we must have an eternal perspective and realize we will one day reap something far greater than anything this earth temporarily offers. The world's temporary means of satisfaction is a counterfeit to what God desires for our lives.

Become a Life-Giver

We can become so exhausted trying to overcome deadly emotion and sin in our own power, only to end up feeling powerless. I know in my own life I've felt powerless at times when dealing with a temptation or sin. It wasn't until I became so sick and tired of my situation, my sinful nature, and having the temptation controlling me that I finally said, *Enough!* Sometimes that's what it takes before we finally say to God, "Help me!" and say to the devil, "Leave me alone!"

What we may forget is that Paul first says to submit ourselves to God, to focus on Christ, and then to resist the devil. It seems easier sometimes to try to do things in our own strength and not rely on God's strength to see us through a situation. But we'll end up being defeated every time. There is no victory apart from God. What I've seen work in my life is to focus less on my sin, less on the temptation, and more on Christ. That is what helps us to overcome the strong passionate desire pulling us in the wrong direction.

Who ultimately brings us life? Jesus! He's the Giver of Life. For us to receive His life and be able to share it, we have to keep ourselves in covenant with Him. When we give in to or even entertain thoughts of lust, we're allowing our flesh to control us instead of asking God to control us. We make choices toward sin instead of choices toward Christ because we are enslaved to the desires controlling us. When we are fully submitted to Christ and His will for us, we are submitting to His plan and desire in exchange for our plans and desires. We become a wellspring of His life that flows out of our covenant relationship with Him.

FREEDOM ACTIONS

1. *Expose the secrets.* What lusts are hidden in your life? Search your heart. Is there any form of lust taking root? Remember, to get freedom, we must be willing to expose the sin we are enslaved to. This brings what was hidden in darkness to the light. Once brought to light, it can be dealt with. All of us are tempted to stay in the dark shadows of the secrets we hold close. Expose the sin in your life by sharing it with someone who loves you beyond your weaknesses and faults, someone who is safe and who practices boundaries in his or her life so your information is kept confidential.

2. *Consecrate or "set apart."* Take steps to set yourself apart from what is enticing you. Everytime you're enticed toward the sinful behavior, take a moment to pray. Ask God to give you strength to go and worship or to go and do something else. Your body is used to having what it craves, whether it's been pornography, food, lovers, material possessions. When you refuse to give in, you'll have to make choices against feelings of want and even desperation. Once your body realizes it's not going to get what it wants and the pleasure center in your brain is retrained to desire new, healthy things of God, the struggling will lessen. When it's tough to set yourself against what you lust after, consider that these things ultimately feed your soul with empty food and increase the desire for more of the same. When you look at pornography, it leaves you feeling shameful, frustrated, and needing more. When you're emotionally distraught

and eat food your body doesn't need, it temporarily satisfies and then you feel distraught again, restless, and looking for something else to feed the void. Step away from counterfeit efforts to fill your longings. Feed your soul with what satisfies—more of Christ!

3. *Accept.* Do other people recognize sinful behaviors in your life? Are there things you long for more than God? Have you gone after these things regardless of the consequences? Get out of denial. It is so hard to admit when we are in sin or when we are tempted by things that appall us. Yet as long as we live in denial, we will continue to be enslaved to the sin. After exposing the sin, we must fully embrace our weakness while treating ourselves with mercy. Yet we also need to face our sin head on. We have to see ourselves as fully accepted through Christ, and we must realize this not just in theory, but in reality. Do we really believe we are loved just as we are? Do we believe and accept we can't overcome without Christ and His strength? We have to rely on *Him,* not on our minds or positive thinking to get beyond the place of sin.

4. *Repent.* Have you brought your lustful desires to the cross? Have you asked God to help you overcome them? Once we have exposed our lust and accepted we are enslaved to it, we must bring it before the Lord and repent of it. If we need to repent daily that's what we'll do until we are no longer enslaved. God knew we would sin when He called us. He knew we would fall in this area, and yet He still loves us. So bring your problem before the One who knows you, who loves you with such deep affection it is unfathomable. He will never leave you or forsake you, even during and after the most horrible muck you can make of your life.

5. *Forgive, forgive, and forgive yourself.* Have you separated yourself from the sin? Have you truly forgiven yourself and given yourself the mercy needed to get beyond it? If you choose not to forgive, you are choosing to be clothed in shame. And shame is another

distraction the enemy will use to keep you from the purposes God
has for your life. Forgive yourself and others so you can walk in the
freedom God offers you. It takes so much energy to hold on to our
past mistakes, our past sin. All the energy we use to hang on to the
junk in our lives is energy we can use to share with others about
God's freedom. Forgive yourself and those who have hurt you.

6. *Press on and be healed.* Are you ready to let it go? Sometimes we continue to hold on to sinful ways because they are habits entrenched
in our lives. They have become such a pattern that we aren't able
to mentally and physically move beyond it. You've probably heard
it said that until the pain of change outweighs the pain of staying
the same, we won't change. This is so true! So renew your mind,
your heart, and your life.

I have the Bible on CD and listen to it every night as I prepare
for bed. This keeps the Word before me every day and helps me to
meditate on and walk in the things God has purposed for me. It
takes radical moves toward God and a radical move away from sin
for us to get free from what enslaves us. Get revolutionary! Allow
God to penetrate your spirit in a new way, a deeper way.

7. *Set boundaries for all relationships.* To keep yourself from getting
into situations you may later have to find a way out of, here are a
few boundaries that may help.

- Keep emails as impersonal as possible without coming
  across as unfriendly or cold. Be brief. Ask yourself
  if the email content is something you could send to
  anyone without regret and if it would seem appropriate
  to someone looking from the outside in.

- Never talk about your partner (husband, wife, boyfriend, girlfriend) negatively.

- Avoid having lunches and dinners with the opposite sex
  alone. When the business conversation ends, it is easy
  to start talking about personal and emotional issues.

- Avoid traveling alone with the opposite sex. Being on the road is one of the most challenging difficulties for relationships. People get lonely and turn to their travel partner for company, which can lead to inappropriate interaction without initially intending it to.

- In any relationship and encounter, ask yourself hard questions: Am I comparing him or her to my spouse? Am I moving my schedule around to see him or her? Am I hiding things from my spouse about this relationship? Am I experiencing emotional connection with him or her?

- If there are warning signs, find a safe person you can confide in who will help you remove yourself from the relationship or situation.

- Avoid flirting. It's hard to know what this looks like for everyone, but it's better to err on the side of caution and know you aren't opening any doors you may have to shut later. Be careful how you interact.

- Avoid intimate conversation about personal thoughts, sex, your fears, or your regrets. These topics open a door to your heart and should be for only our most intimate, godly relationships.

- Don't be afraid to confront someone who is flirting with you, harassing you sexually, or indicating they want to have a closer relationship with you. Be firm and let him or her know you're not interested in going down that road. Make sure to document anything that concerns you and seek counsel if necessary.

- Avoid spiritual intimacy with the opposite sex. When two people who are spiritually passionate about the Lord connect, it's easy to desire a deeper connection. A spiritual connection left unchecked could cross over into a physical relationship or encourage you to invest time, thoughts, and emotions where you shouldn't. This is why we see affairs in churches and ministries. Leadership is not immune to deadly emotions.

Freedom Prayer from Lust

Lord, there is nothing impossible with You. I know this is true, and yet I fail over and over again in this area of my life. It's so difficult to keep pure and holy thoughts and actions in my life. I desire to be faithful to You. Fill my cup with Your truth, Lord. I need You. Help me practice self-control over the lusts that consume me. I want more of You and less of me. Forgive me for filling voids in my life with idols and substitutes for Your love. Help me to run to You when I am craving to be satisfied. Thank You for Your mercy and grace poured over my life. In Jesus' name. Amen.

I have been crucified with Christ.
It is no longer I who live,
but Christ who lives in me.
And the life I now live in the flesh
I live by faith in the Son of God,
who loved me and gave himself for me.

GALATIANS 2:20

6

The Torment of Anger

*Whoever is angry with his brother will be brought to trial,
whoever calls his brother "You good-for-nothing!" will be brought
before the Council, and whoever calls his brother a worthless fool
will be in danger of going to the fire of hell. So if you are about
to offer your gift to God at the altar and there you remember
that your brother has something against you, leave your gift
there in front of the altar, go at once and make peace with your
brother, and then come back and offer your gift to God.*

MATTHEW 5:22-24 TEV

In one of my all-time favorite stories, *Les Misérables,* is a perfect example of an angry man. Officer Javert is ridden with anger his whole life, and eventually reaps the consequences of this deadly emotion. Javert satisfies his anger by strictly enforcing the law with a self-righteousness that is simply a mask for pride. His acceptance of others is based solely on their performance, and he doesn't entertain the notion of grace. Officer Javert holds the same standards for others as he does himself, and he takes great pride in his flawless record and his unwillingness to change his mind or heart about anyone.

Valjean, an ex-convict, was imprisoned for stealing a loaf of bread. After his release, he is again caught stealing, this time from Monseigneur Charles François-Bienvenu Myriel. Bishop Myriel forgives him and covers for him. He tells Valjean that in exchange for this freedom, he must go and live his life and give back to society. A reformed and forgiven Valjean does so quietly but in a way that impacts people and society through all he does.

Javert makes it his life's work to ruin Valjean and expose him for the horrible person he thinks Valjean really is. Javert doesn't believe in the reformation of people, so he sees Valjean as a threat to society. When Valjean proves him wrong over and over, Javert is forced to face this exception. He eventually commits suicide after he is shown compassion and mercy by Valjean.

We don't know what circumstances contributed to Javert being such a heartless, angry man. On the opposite end, in Jean Valjean's circumstances we can see where he might be justified being an angry man. His anger, his unforgiveness, could have consumed him, but instead he chose to love, not just once, but over and over again. Javert had severely beaten Jean Valjean while he was in prison, and in the movie it referred back to those scenes to show the brutality Valjean endured at Javert's hands. When the opportunity came for Valjean to get revenge, we feel Valjean would be justified in killing such a ruthless man. Instead we're treated to a beautiful picture of forgiveness as Valjean continues to forgive and show compassion to Officer Javert.

At the end of the story, Officer Javert, due to his self-righteous beliefs, is unable to accept the mercy of Valjean. The officer finally kills himself to end his torment. Javert was unable to get free from anger in life. He was unable to come to terms with the ongoing anxiety and conflict that was causing him tremendous agony, so he took his own life. Some might say his peace came through his death. But true peace is living and relinquishing the burden of unforgiveness, anger, lust, fear, jealousy, and greed to God and leaving the outcome in His hands. In my opinion, Officer Javert carried the burden himself. He was, in a sense, trying to be his own deliverer, his own god; therefore, he could no longer justify living. He even used his own measure for morality in determining his right to live.

Watching *Les Misérables* touched me so deeply that afterward I went off alone and broke down sobbing. It was such a beautiful picture of the saving grace of Jesus Christ in my own life. Had God based His grace and love for me on my performance I would have been disqualified from forgiveness immediately. I never would have seen the opportunities I have been so blessed to enjoy.

The Root of Anger

Where does anger come from? What typically drives us to anger? For many, it's triggered by one of the other deadly emotions. Levels of anger might be caused by hurt pride, confrontation of a fear, the twinge of jealousy, or the burden of shame. People can easily offend us in areas where we are already wounded, and our past angers can enter our present situation in a flash of emotion.

Anger is "an emotional state that varies in intensity from mild irritation to intense fury and rage," according to Charles Spielberger, Ph.D., a psychologist who specializes in the study of this deadly emotion. Unmet expectation is often at the root of anger. When things don't go as we plan or people don't do what we want them to, our disappointment can lead to different intensities of anger.

Experts encourage us to manage and redirect anger, but what does God's Word say about managing the anger in our lives? God knew people would hurt us, wound us, and betray us. He knew people would lie to us, steal from us, gossip about us. What does He expect of us in these situations? God knew anger would be part of our lives or He wouldn't have addressed it the way He does:

> Know this, my beloved brothers: let every person be quick to hear, slow to speak, slow to anger; for the anger of man does not produce the righteousness that God requires (James 1:19-20).

God tells us to react slowly to situations that might cause the rise of our anger. And then He asks us to be slow to get angry. That sounds logical. We'd buy into that as a general rule of behavior, right? So why is it hard to do those two things when the tidal wave of frustration comes over us and we want to give voice to the rage or hurt we feel? What can we do when anger slams into our hearts?

Unless we're willing to release the people or the incidents in our lives we deem unfair, we will never be free from anger. Our goal is to avoid letting our anger fester, grow, and eventually dominate our lives and the people in our lives. We want to experience freedom and abundance and fulfillment—and live a whole, fulfilling life.

> Be angry and do not sin; do not let the sun go down on your anger, and give no opportunity to the devil (Ephesians 4:26).

Anger Surrendered

A simmering anger lies right below the surface for some people—an anger that goes undetected until triggered. Let's look at Tom, an example of the impact of brewing, stewing anger.

Tom had outbursts of anger that were triggered by situations with his wife or kids. But *what* they did or said was not the *source* of his anger. He was mad at and disappointed in himself. He'd spent years living a secret life that involved delving into pornography and prostitution. Because he had so much disgust for himself, simmering anger was constant and always ready to explode. One day while waiting for his wife, Barbara, to come out of the store, he suddenly lost his patience and decided her time for shopping was up. She'd only been in the store for five minutes, but to Tom it was five minutes too long. He marched into the store fuming, walked up to the counter where she was checking out, and unleashed the anger he'd been holding in. This wasn't a response to the situation at hand; it was a response to years of self-loathing. Barbara stood there humiliated and her own anger rose. This wasn't the first time Tom berated her. He'd been doing this for years to her and the children.

Would you be friends with someone like Tom? Would you acquiesce to his outbursts of anger at home or at work? In Tom's case, he held back his strong wrath at work. In fact, if someone at work were asked, they would say Tom was one of the most polite, friendly men they knew. I spoke with a domestic abuse counselor, and she shared that this is often the case with those who are abusive. They present charming personalities in the workplace and even with their families and spouses when necessary. But their dark side is very dark. Their anger is poison, and when unleashed, the venom is lethal. By squelching his anger during the day, Tom saved a mighty rush of it for his family when he got home.

For Tom to surrender his anger he would have to surrender control. Most of us struggle with the surrender of control part, but when faced with losing our families or our hope for the purpose God intended, hopefully most of us would wake up to the necessity of giving our lives over to God's care. Once we confess and reveal our anger—the unforgiveness and bitterness that rage inside us—we can walk a new path.

Arresting the Anger

Whenever I sense an injustice is being done to me, I take the dark thoughts that go with my hurt and sort through them. I begin to speak truth in my mind to counter and calm those negative thoughts. Usually I discover that my interpretation of injustice isn't warranted in the situation. I find that I have misunderstood what someone has said or done and perceived it as a personal attack when it wasn't intended as one. Have you faced similar times of overreacting to life because of a trail of dark thoughts? Our first impressions and instincts are often based on a skewed understanding of truth and justice.

One of my sons used to play the victim a lot when he was little. If he didn't get his way, he would say, "Mom, you don't love me. You don't even care about me." I knew I had to correct this thinking or he would go through his years being the victim, meaning his focus would be on him. "I didn't get this" or "I didn't get that." When anger develops based on feelings of *perceived* injustice or a constant whine of "Woe is me," it becomes a setup for unhappiness and a permanent state of dissatisfaction and anger. So when my son cried "Injustice," I asked him to describe what he was feeling. I asked him questions to help him realize he was believing lies, not truths. When he challenged my love for him, I'd walk him through the truths that he was well aware of: I do love him. I do care for him. His anger and his excuses eventually passed, and, in time, he was able to avoid the negativity of his "the whole world is against me" syndrome.

The same is true for us. Haven't we complained about something happening at home or work and promptly shifted the blame for our feelings onto someone else? When feelings of injustice or anger well up, immediately begin to ask yourself questions that will help you walk from lies to truth. You'll avoid impulsive, negative reactions and be basing your responses to people and trials and life circumstances on reality. Here are a few questions to get you started:

1. Why do I feel this way?
2. Will getting angry change the situation for the better?
3. Will my anger cause irreparable damage to someone?
4. What are these feelings really about?
5. When have I felt this way before?
6. What does God's Word say about this situation?
7. Do I need to forgive someone?
8. Who should really be in charge of the outcome of this situation?
9. Do I need to show unconditional love to someone?
10. What gift or lesson from God will I miss if I let anger have control?

How exaggerated our thoughts can be at times. When we do gain a more godly perspective, these start to seem a bit crazy. However, what about when our thoughts, hurts, and sense of injustice are valid? What then? We can't write them off as believing a lie, and we can't dismiss them as mere negative thinking. We still ask ourselves the questions just listed. While the injustice might be true, our line of thought might still be based on lies or the wounds of past (heart bruises) rather than the actual scenario happening today.

I've felt unloved at times and even said, "You don't really love me.

You don't even care about me." And what I should have done before those words came out of my mouth was ask myself whether they were true. Am I really not loved by this person? Does this person really not care about me? If it is true, what is the best way to *respond* so I'm not attacking the other person? This isn't easy. We need mental discipline, but it is well worth the freedom from being controlled by anger and the sin we engage in as a result.

Why Anger Consumes

We've all lashed out in anger. These regrettable moments sometimes haunt us for years. What is it about anger that stays with us? What have we allowed in our lives? What anger are we holding on to? If God has given us grace and forgiveness in the areas of our lives where we've failed, are we not to extend that same grace and mercy to others? When we lean on our understanding of how people should be judged, we can easily end up expressing anger toward them, as well as unforgiveness. In our *Les Misérables* example, Javert did this to Valjean.

Forgiving when we feel justified, when we feel someone has wronged us and they deserve to be punished, is difficult. It's tough to rest in God's handling of the situation, especially if we feel like God isn't handling it the way *we* would if we were in control. If we take matters into our own hands and decide to punish through anger, we aren't actually punishing the offender. How are they paying for what they've done when we are the ones sinking into the pit of anger? And our lack of forgiveness is not revealing and extending to them God's grace.

I have met so many wives who haven't forgiven their former spouses. Some have been divorced for 20 years and are still wearing raw bitterness clothing. Bitterness begins in the heart, but the evidence of it is eventually expressed in our demeanor. When you meet them they spew out the injustices of their perpetrators as if putting them on trial over and over again.

One of the saddest aspects of this prolonged anger from divorce is that the former spouses of these women still control them. These women will be tied to all the emotions and injustices they felt when their heartbreaks were new as long as they hold on to the bitterness. I met a divorced couple, and they spewed the most horrible cuss words at one another every time they spoke. They seemed to take pleasure in hurting each other. I counseled the woman to forgive, and she began to take steps toward releasing the anger and the hurt while finding ways to also let go of this man who had wronged her. Today they are able to speak cordially to each other. They have both softened and moved on with their lives, but it took surrendering their control, their wills, and their power to God for the change to take place. Is there someone you're holding in contempt? Someone you have not forgiven?

> "In your anger do not sin": Do not let the sun go down while you are still angry, and do not give the devil a foothold (Ephesians 4:26-27 NIV).

In Anger Siblings Sell Brother

In the midst of anger and hate, we're usually putting most of our attention on the one who has offended us. We most likely don't consider what we may have done to provoke the offense. In Genesis 37, the story of Jacob's favorite son, Joseph, and his older brothers is told. This story of anger, betrayal, and forgiveness is so popular that a Broadway play was made of it! Joseph was 17 when he took a bad report about his brothers and their work habits to his father. Nobody likes a tattletale, and the brothers were angry because of Joseph's disloyalty. Then their father gave Joseph a special gift—a beautiful coat of many colors—because he loved Joseph so much and favored him. And we know those brothers were paying close attention to this special treatment of their brother! They weren't pleased.

When Joseph had a couple of interesting dreams, he felt compelled to share them with his brothers. In the context of the dreams, he shared how one day his brothers would bow down to him. Now I'm sure Joseph meant well as he shared his God-given dreams, but he was basically stating that God told him he would one day rule over his brothers. Can you imagine their hostility? *Say what?* they probably thought. First, the father showed favoritism toward Joseph, and now Joseph was claiming that even God favored him. This deepened the brothers' hate. Overcome with anger and jealousy, the brothers sold Joseph into slavery. Many years later Joseph was able to say to them, "You plotted evil against me, but God turned it to good" (Genesis 50:20). God used and redeemed the anger-influenced actions of the brothers to bring about great things. You see, it was never Joseph's job, responsibility, or purpose to punish his brothers for their behavior. He gave his emotions and the situation to God and with that act of surrender came forgiveness and restoration. God is amazing! I encourage you to read this story start to finish for inspiration.

The Power to Forgive

I've had to forgive a lot of offenses in my life. As a young teenager I experienced date rape, and later in life I was raped again by someone who forced his way into my house. The fear from these violent acts was difficult to give to God, but I think the hardest thing I've ever had to let go of and release to the Lord was my anger and pain from my divorce.

I didn't want the divorce; there had never been a divorce in my family. I had witnessed firsthand my parents' marriage endure and overcome great trials, and I felt sure my husband and I could do the same if we were willing. But that wasn't the outcome. I was devastated and angry at my husband and at God.

I knew I had to make the choice to take my eyes off of what I *felt* my husband had done to me and focus on what I needed to change. I had to ask myself hard questions, such as how I could have provoked him and what I could have and should have done differently. None of us wants to look at our responsibility when things go wrong. We want to shift the blame or stay in denial of our own sin, but this hinders our growth in Christ and keeps us from intimate relationship with Him. If I remained in my anger I'd be tormented by feelings of injustice, and those feelings would eventually lead to bitterness and hardness of heart. If my heart is shut down to others, I'll also be shutting my relationship with God off as well.

My anger didn't leave as soon as I prayed about it and asked myself those hard evaluation questions we looked at earlier. I had to *pursue* forgiveness and work at actively forgiving my former husband. I had to have a determination in me that was strengthened and carried by the work of the Holy Spirit in my life. It wasn't in my strength to forgive, but by the power of the Holy Spirit I was able to find victory in this area. What I did control was my answer to God when He asked me, "Will you forgive those who have betrayed you, persecuted you, abused you, condemned you, shamed you, forgotten you, abandoned you?" My answer was and is, "Yes, Lord." I say yes. What do you say? I stayed angry for a time, but the more I focused on my sins and shortcomings and my future hope in Christ, the less angry I was with my husband and the easier it was to forgive any offenses that had taken place.

My anger from my divorce eventually stirred up past memories of relationships that had also wounded my heart. That old anger rushed afresh in my veins. I knew enough to know that if I didn't deal with my hurts, my unresolved anger, my unmet expectations, and even my own hurtful actions, I would hand down anger to my kids and carry my anger into future relationships and friendships. I had to face the pain head on and deal with the truth. For five years I worked through areas in my life I felt were unresolved, and as the healing came, my anger left. It wasn't easy for me to forgive my husband, nor was it easy to look at areas where I could have responded in a better way. But I knew for my healing and my restoration I had to do both.

I have people tell me quite often how amazed they are at the relationship I have with my former spouse and the father of my four kids. He even helped me in the writing of this book by getting our kids where they needed to go or taking them out when I needed to write. None of this would have been possible if I hadn't obeyed God's Word. I had a choice: to believe God's Word was true or not to believe. I chose to lean on His understanding even though I felt justified to hate, justified to not forgive, justified to continue to hang on to all that was done to me. I chose the cross over my pride. As hard as this choice was, for the sake of my children, for the sake of my relationship with Jesus, I chose God's way over my way and allowed Him to deal with the outcomes.

As a Christian, there is really only one choice: embracing the act of forgiveness and the decision to not be angry. Initially this may be a choice we make mentally, but our hearts will follow suit when they are healed and ready to do so. This is a long process for some and an instantaneous happening for others. To live in denial and pretend we aren't angry is as harmful as the anger itself. Just like every other deadly emotion, exposure is key. Walking through the release of it is secondary.

> Never take revenge, my friends, but instead let God's anger do it. For the scripture says, "I will take revenge, I will pay back, says the Lord" (Romans 12:19 TEV).

Exchange God's Truth for the Lies of Anger

My sister used to joke with me that I was attracted to the bad apples in the world. One day I commented back and told her that sometimes we have to experience the bad apples to find the good ones. She responded, "Well, yes…maybe. But no one has to go through a whole bag." I had my share of bad apples along the way. I found out later in life my gifts of mercy and compassion can be detriments if not handled with care. They called it "missionary dating" when I was a kid—probably still do.

One boy I dated (I'll call him Mike) was a very angry soul. He'd grown up with a stepfather who was heavy-handed and gave Mike little affirmation. Mike probably came into the world fighting. He seemed to think the entire world was against him. I just knew I would be the first person to believe in him and help him change. My compassion went out to his situation, and I felt I could help him overcome all the bad things that had happened to him along life's way.

Sound familiar? Many of us, especially women, find ourselves in relationships that are all about rescuing another person. God taught me after a few rescues that only He is God, and I was not to play Savior. It took a while for me to realize I was filling my own need of being needed by playing hero. If you're someone who also tends to rescue people in relationships, ask yourself why.

Mike and I dated for a year. The first few months we had a wonderful friendship. He needed my affirmation and I needed to play hero. He seemed to trust me. But over time his trust faded. He became extremely possessive, humiliating me in public because of his insecurities. Mike didn't love or trust himself, so he couldn't trust me. Why would I love him? How could I love him?

He would discourage my friendships, and if I even had a conversation with another boy, he would fly into a rage. I felt sorry for Mike, but even though I was young and naïve I knew that the problem was way beyond me. Mike hated himself. He hated life. He hated, he hated, he hated. And while he hated, he pretended to be a confident young man, but inside he was a scared little boy masking his insecurities with this tough boy image. In case someone picked a fight with him, he carried a weapon around. He started threatening those who tried to speak to me or who spoke to him in a way he felt was threatening. He lived in one mode—anger. He always thought the very worst of people, and before he even had a chance to get to know them, he disqualified them before they disqualified him.

Mike's anger worked well on the wrestling mat. He won a state championship in high school, but he would never go on to college because he didn't believe he was good enough. Our relationship finally came to an end. After a year of dealing with his anger and abusive personality, my parents demanded I end the relationship. My mom had seen Mike push me in the yard when we were in a heated discussion, and after that he was never allowed at my house again. Mom detected Mike's problem early on and warned me, but you know how it can be at that age. I was sure she was wrong. She'd grown up with an alcoholic father who was physically abusive and very similar to Mike. He also believed the world was against him, and no matter what happened or what anyone said, he never believed someone could love him or accept him.

Some years later I had a chance to talk to Mike for a brief moment. I quickly realized he hadn't changed a bit. I'd become a Christian and felt prompted to share with him the love of Christ, but he would hear nothing of it. He was angry with God and had no desire to hear about what it meant to have a relationship with Him.

Mike was an extreme case of what anger can do and how it can control and rule your life. According to a 1998 U.S. Department of Justice and the Commonwealth Fund report, 31 percent of American women report being abused by a spouse or boyfriend. Worldwide, at least one in three women have been beaten, coerced into sex, or otherwise abused. Why is there so much anger, and how do we keep ourselves safe?

What are the lies Mike believed that caused him to live his life with such vehement anger? What are the lies we believe that cause us to live with anger and that lead us to inflict our anger onto others?

Lie #1: It is my right to be angry. We may believe it is our right to be angry. We are justified because our expectations have not been met. Somewhere along the way, Mike was hurt very deeply. He doesn't believe in God and hasn't embraced the principle of forgiveness.

The truth: God is a loving God. His ways are not our ways. But we can rest in the knowledge that He is our advocate. We can trust Him with everything in our lives, including our circumstances and anger. We will face trials and disappointments, but God promises He will never leave us or forsake us.

> I will say to the Lord, "My refuge and my fortress, my God, in whom I trust" (Psalm 91:2).

Lie #2: Anger will help me to feel better about the situation.
The truth: Anger hurts everyone in or near the situation when it

is acted out in violence. It hurts us deeply. It impacts those around us deeply. We can't excuse our anger by calling it necessary or warranted. Yes, there are times we are right to be incensed about an injustice or harm that has come to people or a nation. But the initial anger that might inspire good change is never meant to be a foundation for living.

Lie #3: Being angry will change the situation and make the other person pay.

The truth: Anger doesn't change the wrong that has occurred or fill expectations. Instead, it opens our hearts to unforgiveness and bitterness so we aren't able to receive forgiveness from God or pass it along to others. Unforgiveness becomes an obstacle between you and the God you serve.

> They are darkened in their understanding and separated from the life of God because of the ignorance that is in them due to the hardening of their hearts (Ephesians 4:18 NIV).

Lie #4: If we have a good reason, it's okay to harbor anger.

The truth: As believers there are no reasons that justify remaining in anger toward another person. Jesus instructs us to *love* our enemies and *bless* those who persecute us. This makes no sense to the world, but to a believer it is the only way we can continue to walk free of bitterness.

> I say to you that everyone who is angry with his brother will be liable to judgment; whoever insults his brother will be liable to the council; and whoever says, "You fool!" will be liable to the hell of fire (Matthew 5:22).

The Deadly Consequences of Anger

In their bestselling book *Anger Kills,* authors Redford and Virginia Williams state that studies support the theory that anger is not just a negative emotion but something that can also kill. Anger can lead to heart disease, heart attacks, heart rhythm irregularities, and many other life-threatening diseases. The authors point out that a person who fails to recognize and deal with his or her anger is just like someone who takes a small dose of a poison each day. Eventually the entire system becomes toxic and literally leads to death.

> "In your anger do not sin": Do not let the sun go down while
> you are still angry (Ephesians 4:26 NIV).

Anger, the emotion, is inevitable, but to allow anger to become rooted in your life and mind and heart and soul will lead to sin. There is no way to cloak part of your life in such darkness and move toward God's light. Your defenses will weaken, your thoughts will spiral, and your emotions will become even more toxic.

Possible Results of Anger

> Get rid of all bitterness, rage and anger, brawling and slander,
> along with every form of malice. Be kind and compassionate
> to one another, forgiving each other, just as in Christ God
> forgave you (Ephesians 4:31-32 NIV).

Bitterness

Bitterness is really a result of toxic hatred. It's what happens when we allow anger and unforgiveness to fester and develop into intense dislike or hatred for someone. Bitterness has been known to affect a person's health physically and emotionally, and it definitely shows on a person's countenance. If we have truly forgiven someone, we will pray for blessing on him or her. Bitterness becomes a prison and a poison: "Guard against turning back from the grace of God. Let no one become like a bitter plant that grows up and causes many troubles with its poison" (Hebrews 12:15-16 TEV).

Rage

When we move into rage, we let feelings overtake us. Rage can cause us to move toward sinful behavior as we become out of control and reckless. When we allow anger to take root and bitterness to set in, rage is easily triggered. This is why we have to cut off anger and unforgiveness at the roots, at the very beginning stages, because once it sets in, it's like a tree whose roots have gone deep: Pulling it out takes a lot more force than if it's pulled out and destroyed when it's an acorn.

Harsh Words

Life and death are found in the power of the tongue. It's so easy to spew out the ugliness that overtakes us when we're angry and when we're hurt. How many times have we said things we regret? Words we can never take back. Our mouths pour out venom that destroys, tears down, rips apart, and even kills in ways we aren't even fully aware of. If we've released someone and forgiven them, we will not talk about them in a negative manner. We will not tell them over and over what they did or correct them in front of others. We will not argue our point, but we will love them even if we don't agree with them. "A gentle answer quiets anger, but a harsh one stirs it up" (Proverbs 15:1 TEV).

> It is to a man's honor to avoid strife, but every fool is quick to quarrel (Proverbs 20:3 NIV).

Slander

"People with a hot temper do foolish things; wiser people remain calm" (Proverbs 14:17 TEV). How many opportunities have there been in our lives to slander someone we dislike—maybe someone who wronged us, betrayed us—rather than leave the results up to God? Tearing down those we despise is easy. Destroying with our words and our gossip and our spewing hate language is easier than forgiving. If we haven't truly forgiven, we will slander people behind their backs or perhaps in front of them as a way to get revenge. This is so destructive to the body of Christ. What we really want is healing. But in the time following pain and suffering, we mistakenly believe anger will protect us and eventually heal us through revenge. Think before you say something about someone's reputation. Don't be quick to judge when you don't know the details. God will most certainly hold us accountable for our words.

The Fruit of the Spirit Overcomes Anger

> Be imitators of God, as beloved children. And walk in love, as Christ loved us and gave himself up for us, a fragrant offering and sacrifice to God (Ephesians 5:1).

Angry people are impatient. They spew anger everywhere and cause division wherever they go. Patience is the fruit of the Spirit that will help us overcome anger and agitation. What actions can we take to move toward patience? Imagine taking deep breaths instead of fuming over having to wait in line. Consider getting to know someone rather than rushing by them. Impatience eats away at our characters, our beliefs, and our hopes. It creates a path for anger to seep into the way we approach little things, such as the way other people drive or the way we interact with strangers. When we practice patience in small and big ways, soon it will become our first response when we face trials, irritations, and potentially anger-infusing situations. Patience covers us even when we face the anger of others. We don't feel compelled to join in or return anger for anger, sin for sin.

> Repay no one evil for evil, but give thought to do what is honorable in the sight of all. If possible, so far as it depends on you, live peaceably with all (Romans 12:17-18).

Become a Life-Giver

> Hatred stirs up strife, but love covers all offenses (Proverbs 10:12).

The tragic shooting of 10 Amish girls in a one-room school in October 2006 brought reporters throughout the world to Lancaster County, PA, to cover the terrible event. But the story reporters set out to write took an unexpected turn. I'm sure they planned on doing interviews with people whose lives would be in complete chaos and who were filled with anger toward the killer and God. Instead they found a community grieving over their shocking losses and expressing grief, forgiveness, and sorrow for the family of the man who pulled the trigger and killed their innocent, beautiful daughters.

The world was astounded by this amazing display of forgiveness. The Amish community refused to cast blame; instead, they modeled forgiveness. They didn't immediately question why this tragedy happened or why God would allow it. They didn't call the media and hold a press conference with attorneys at their sides. They didn't point fingers. No, they reached out with grace and compassion to the killer's family.

On the very afternoon of the tragedy, the grandfather of one of the girls who was killed expressed forgiveness toward Charles Roberts, the man who was responsible for their horrific deaths. The Amish community expressed forgiveness and sorrow for the Roberts family and, later that week, an invitation was extended to the Roberts family to attend the funeral of one of the Amish girls. But the Amish's love and compassion didn't stop there. The Amish believers out-numbered the non-Amish at Charles Roberts' funeral.

Such grace and forgiveness was foreign to the killer. Unforgiveness and anger tormented Charles Roberts. He'd lost his daughter to premature death and had never forgiven God. Yet after Roberts killed 10 Amish school girls, the Amish not only forgave Charles Roberts, but extended grace and compassion to his family, telling them they would not be shamed in the community but were forgiven.

In the midst of a world filled with war, terrorism, and people who point fingers, shift blame, and are eager to sue for the slightest offense, this was truly unheard of. The world was wondering, the press was bewildered. How could a people struck with such grief and tragedy, such loss and violence against innocent lives, forgive such an act and not look for someone to pay? Jesus was their answer, and He is ours too. We may not understand Him at times ourselves. The grave injustices in the world are never ending, but we act in obedience to the principles our Christian belief is founded on. Love and forgiveness are our life themes. We understand we have been forgiven so much, we have been excused much, and in turn we extend forgiveness to others so we won't fall into the prison of bitterness and defeat.

Jesus, as He hung on the cross in the greatest despair after being humiliated, spit on, rejected, and betrayed, whispered, "Father, forgive them, for they know not what they do" (Luke 23:34). What would we be thinking while hanging on that cross? What do we think when someone wrongs us now? Are we recounting the numerous offenses against us? Are we seeking an eye for an eye judgment? Do we want those who have offended us to pay a steep price? These choices keep us under the law and reflect a life without Christ. They yield emotional, spiritual, and even physical death to those who follow them. Christ said, "Blessed are the merciful, for they shall receive mercy" (Matthew 5:7).

When we're angry all the time, how are we affecting others? Are we giving life or are we robbing people of it? When we walk around bitter and full of complaints, how does this bring life to ourselves, to our families and friends, and to other people? Examine your anger right now and take a close look at what it is stealing from you. When was the last time you felt peace inside? Whether you experience brief instances of intense emotion and overreactions or you function in a daily mode of anger, you are missing out on a life ruled by God's peace. Begin releasing your anger to God. God wants you to be free so you can begin to share His life with those around you.

No one wants to be around angry, bitter, unhappy people. You may not be totally cut off yet, but ultimately you're robbing yourself of intimate relationships because people aren't able to be really honest with their feelings. They're too afraid of your responses. They walk on eggshells around you and engage in a shallow relationship because there is little truth, little accountability, and little community. I have seen an entire household revolve around one angry person, and that person controls whether the family has peace or not. Stop being a peace robber and begin to give life to yourself and others.

═══ FREEDOM ACTIONS ═══

1. *Let go of past regret and failure.* In so many instances I've seen people direct their anger toward God and themselves due to failures in life. Release your failures to Christ. Ask Him to heal those painful memories, those flaws, those failings, and free you from guilt and pain. Write down ways you have grown spiritually and emotionally as a result of those failures. Bitter or better is always the choice. Even if you've chosen bitter in the past, choose to get better today. It's never too late!

2. *Acknowledge the anger is real.* As a believer it's easy to think, *I can't be angry because I am a Christian.* To deny the feeling of anger when people hurt you isn't based on truth. You are not superhuman. God never said you are to never be angry. He said not to sin during your anger. Acknowledge you are angry and allow Jesus to begin a good work in your heart. He will heal the pain if you open yourself to being set free. Every day spend time in worship, allowing it to soften your heart. Maintaining a hardened heart is very difficult when you listen to worship music every day. I've tried this, and it really works to open your heart back up to God and to your loved ones.

3. *Repent.* I know I've said this in just about every chapter, but it's so significant and true! When we repent of our sin, God begins our healing. When we repent of anger, we are acknowledging our dependence on God to overcome this deadly emotion.

4. *Forgive.* Why do you think Jesus said to forgive 70 times 7? Jewish tradition called for individuals to forgive 3 times, so when Jesus responded they should forgive 70 times 7, He was saying to them that forgiveness is unending. We must extend forgiveness to others over and over again, in the same way we go to Christ over and over again when we sin. There have only been a couple times when I

just didn't know how I could ever forgive what was done to me. To gain perspective, I concentrated on the ugliness of my own sin so I could forgive the one who wronged me. This helped me have mercy and compassion for the other person.

5. *Pray over your anger and lay it at the altar.* Ask God to help you in your journey to overcome this deadly emotion. Ask Him to reveal to you what has caused your deep anger or even your irritability and actions of anger. Seek God's presence in prayer so He can reveal what sometimes is not even evident—the deep secrets of your heart. Sometimes we are completely unaware of why we are angry. Prayer and meditation prepare us to hear God's answers and revelations about ourselves and whatever He requires of us. Take moments for silence. Sit and listen and, more importantly, hear what God has to say to you. He is faithful to those who pursue healing. He is the healer of your emotions and your physical ailments.

6. *Exercise self-control.* Be slow to react and wait until the anger subsides before responding. Pray for self-control before you need it. Protect yourself from your own irrational responses—mental and physical—by practicing self-control and patience.

7. *Keep your expectations realistic.* Don't expect people to fill your emotional needs. They will fail you, and they will disappoint you—just as you fail and disappoint others. Release the disappointment and resentment so you don't sin in your anger. Expect the best in people, but don't expect perfection. Lean on God as you work through your pain and your anger because He is here for you. And don't rely on your own willpower to counter years of built up anger. You were not made to change your own heart. Let God truly be God in your life.

Freedom Prayer from Anger

Lord, forgive me for sinning in my anger. I cry out to You for mercy. Please renew my mind and transform my heart. Peel away the layers of hardness that have built up through the sins of my bitterness and unforgiveness. Please strengthen me and help me forgive those who have wounded me. Forgive me for wounding others…and You…in my anger. Lord, help me adopt Your principles in my life. Give me the strength and wisdom to be slow to speak, slow to anger, and to not sin when I am angry. Thank You for delivering me from the anguish that rages in my soul. I need Your living water to flow through me. Holy Spirit, replenish me. Cause love to pour from my heart and into the lives of people around me. In Jesus' name. Amen.

Know this, my beloved brothers:
let every person be quick to hear, slow to speak,
slow to anger; for the anger of man does not
produce the righteousness that God requires.

JAMES 1:19

7

The Burden of Stress

*Ask yourself these two questions: (1) "What problems are in
my hands today?" You can probably think of several pressing
issues pretty quickly—things that your mind is drawn to
whenever it has some down time; and (2) "What does God
hold in His hands today?" The answer, of course, is the
whole world. Everything. Think about that. If you let go of
what's in your hands, whose hands will it be in? God's.*

Chip Ingram

Stress contributes to life-threatening problems such as heart attack, stroke, depression, infection, and chronic aches and pains. Its weight can hold us back from freedom living. While stress is not the actual emotion felt (many times people feel anxiety and distress), it is frequently the direct result of deadly emotions manifested in our lives. Our lives are complex, and many of us stay so busy trying to survive the demands of each day that we don't take time to recognize our stress or deal with it in a healthy way.

Jesus reminded us to cast all our cares upon Him: "Come to me, all you who are weary and burdened, and I will give you rest. Take my yoke upon you and learn from me, for I am gentle and humble in heart, and you will find rest for your souls. For my yoke is easy and my burden is light" (Matthew 11:28-30 NIV). Is stress a burden? Absolutely! And it comes in lots of forms. Chances are that you're experiencing stress right now on many levels and triggered by multiple factors. You may be lumping everything into one category and cry, "I'm so stressed!" It's good to explore the specific causes of your stress so you can delve into God's solutions for those particular areas.

The Root of Stress

Where does stress come from? Ask 10 people and you'll discover 10 sources of stress. I have two friends who are each currently carrying the financial burden of their households. Their husbands are out of jobs, and these women temporarily play the roles of providers, wives, and mothers. They have little energy or resources left for themselves. One feels she can barely hold up the load. The burden is taking a huge toll on her marriage, the family, and on my friend's health. She is starting to lose her hair and has taken to drinking extremely strong coffee drinks to keep up her energy level. Both women have demanding jobs that require at least 12-hour days. They are keeping up the maintenance on large homes and trying to hold everything else together as well.

The stress of finances probably is familiar. Whether we're living on two incomes, surviving as a single parent, or able to be a stay-at-home mom, the amount of responsibility and demands placed on us can be overwhelming.

What is the root of stress? New job, new home, bigger retirement, our child's future, pregnancy, the loss of a family member or friend, new relationships, marriage...the list goes on forever. We can also be stressed over daily life tasks such as driving, kids' commitments to sports, our social engagements, keeping up the home. The demands of life are enough to stress us out daily. So how can we manage that stress and keep peace in our lives?

Stress Surrendered

Worry doesn't change our circumstances. Only God is capable of really giving us peace in the midst of chaos. Surrendering all our cares to Him isn't easy. It should be, but somehow it feels like we're preventing bad things from happening if we keep worrying about money, kids, the future, work, our to-do list, and so on. We know as Christians that God has things in control, that He holds us in His hands, but do we really believe with our minds and trust with our hearts that He is going to take care of us?

Come to me, all who labor and are heavy laden, and I will give you rest (Matthew 11:28).

Mistress Bares Child and Is Cast Out

The Lord God made a covenant with Abram and gave him a vision showing him that his descendents would be as numerous as the stars in the sky. At the time his wife, Sarai, had no children, and Abram didn't have an heir. But he believed God would give him and Sarai a child.

As time went on, Sarai was still barren and, even though God had made it clear she would bear a child, the older she became the less she believed it. She asked Abram to lie with her maidservant, Hagar, so she could have a child through a surrogate. Abram said yes, and he did as Sarai asked. But once the child was born, Sarai was jealous and drove Hagar and her babe out of the community.

God would bless the child of Hagar, but His *covenant* would be with Sarai's child. God changed Sarai to Sarah. He changed Abram's name to Abraham, and gave His word to him that he and Sarah would have a child. By this time Abraham was 100 years old, and he couldn't imagine how God could make true on His promise. Sarah even laughed when she heard what God had spoken. But sure enough, God kept His word and the following year they had little Isaac.

Abraham and Sarah had both been consumed with worry for different reasons. Abraham wanted a son to carry on his heritage. Sarah wanted to bear her husband a child and meet the standards of the day. Sarah's concern caused her to go to Hagar and ask her to bear a child for her and Abraham. Her worry caused her more pain because once Hagar had the child, Sarah felt even more humiliated and broken.

More stress was created because Abraham and Sarah strayed from the plan and purpose God had revealed to them. How many times do we go before God and ask Him for direction and guidance...and then get so impatient, so stressed that we jump ahead with *our* plans, *our* intentions? We handle life with what we see and know instead of trusting how He will orchestrate it.

Why We Stress Out

> Therefore I tell you, do not be anxious about your life, what
> you will eat or what you will drink, nor about your body,
> what you will put on. Is not life more than food, and the
> body more than clothing? (Matthew 6:25).

As believers in Christ, why do we stress and feel anxious? Are we really trusting in God or are we leaning on our own understanding the way Abraham and Sarah did? God still blessed them, just like He will continue to be here for us with open arms even during our biggest mistakes. He'll use what is bad in our lives for something good and He'll forgive us. But just imagine what would happen if we trusted Him with all our worries, all our mistakes, and all the painful disappointments? What amazing things could come about if we learned to trust Him through all things and believe Him in all things!

One night while talking with a friend, I began to share some of my greatest fears and the stress I was experiencing as a result. Carrying the burden of finances, children, and everything else had peaked, and I was feeling extremely overwhelmed. My friend patiently listened to me and then looked me in the eye and said, "Michelle, God is enough." "Hmmm?" I questioned, as if I hadn't heard him right. "God is enough? What do you mean?" I asked. And he responded, "As believers, our trust is in Christ, and if it is in Christ, He is enough for us no matter what happens."

What a simple statement—but such a profound one. God is enough. He is enough for me, and He is enough for you. Allowing stress to control us and destroy us doesn't help the situation, it only worsens it. So let it go. Release the stress and worry to God. Pursue the one in control, and His peace will surpass all understanding. We are limited in what we know, but God is unlimited!

God's Truth for the Lies of Stress

Lie #1: God only helps those who help themselves. I had a friend repeat this over and over to me. There have been many times when I didn't do exactly as I should have, and God did a miraculous work in my circumstances.

The truth: The idea that God only helps us if we do something, if we perform in some way, is a lie. God's great love for us is unconditional. If Christ lives in us and abides with us, He is present in *every* moment of our lives. He won't leave us or abandon us, even in our times of weakness and trouble. When we reach to Him for help, He is here, ready and able and willing to respond. He *never* leaves us or forsakes us! God is faithful even when we are not. We can rely on His strength, not our own to keep us on track...or get us back on track. Through Him we can pursue our healing, through Him we can overcome the demons tearing us apart, through Him we can do all things.

> If we are faithless, He remains faithful—for he cannot deny himself (2 Timothy 2:13).

Lie #2: God doesn't care—He has too many other things to worry about. God can't possibly be interested in the mundane and minute details of our lives.

The truth: God is here for you at all times. "But even the hairs of your head are all numbered. Fear not, therefore; you are of more value than many sparrows" (Matthew 10:29-30). God doesn't just know how many hairs we have on our heads, He also knows when we can't pay the bills, when our children need something and we can't provide it, and when our spouse is not treating us fairly. When we go to God with our cares, He is then able to show His glory in our situation. He cares about even the smallest things that are important to us. He wants to be involved in who we are and what is important to us. This doesn't mean the outcomes of our situations will always be what we want. This is where trusting in His purpose and plan comes into play. We'll experience disappointments and unmet expectations. And, believe it or not, this is where joy comes from! Out of the suffering and pain comes the sweetness of joy as our desperate need for God is revealed.

It is an incredible moment when we finally believe that we can rest in Him as our Lord.

God demonstrates His sovereignty over His creation; He is never asleep at the switch. He is right there for us at all times. He knew before we did that we would lose the job we'd been with for 20 years, when a child almost died in the hospital of pneumonia, and that we would make a mistake by spending more than we make. He knew, He knows, and He provides, giving us peace in the midst of our shattered dreams.

> *Thou has formed us for thyself, and our hearts*
> *are restless till they find rest in thee.*
>
> ST. AUGUSTINE

Lie #3: The more I concern myself with things, the more I'm in control.
The truth: We feel a false sense of comfort when we try to be in control. Of course, we never really are in control; it's just an illusion. But if we operate under this illusion, we're saying we don't trust God for the outcome of our lives. God has given us the ability to prepare, to make plans, to work, and yet to remain open to His purpose and plan for our lives. In the midst of it all, God is in control.

Deadly Consequences of Stress

In the New King James Version the word "peace" is mentioned more than 300 times. Obviously peace is something God very much wants us to attain in this life. Not only does He share in His Word that He wants to give us peace, but He also makes it clear He is the God of peace.

We may wonder how it is even possible to attain peace when we feel overworked most of the time, when life seems impossible to balance, when the world around us seems chaotic with war and political unrest. If we read through God's Word, we'll find that the same things were taking place throughout history. God's people have often lived in a state of stress rather than in the peace God calls them to and offers openly. Why do we resist this offering of peace?

What happens to us when we allow things, people, and situations, to rob us of our peace? What are we all in search for? Inner peace is something most people long for. Here are just a few of the deadly consequences we may experience when we live a life of stress and disorder.

We make important decisions while anxious. When we operate from a life that is not peaceful or peace filled, we're making many decisions in a negative and unhealthy way that impact our families and us. We also become very distracted from our relationship with Christ. We find ourselves paralyzed, unable to walk in faith and experience God in a full way. As time goes on and the stresses build, we make more and more decisions apart from God's wisdom. We think in terms of fear, not faith.

We create chaos and disorder. Anytime there is unhealthy stress in our lives, a lot of us experience inner chaos from which we in turn create a world of disorder around us. Have you ever been so scattered with work and kids and life demands that soon your living room or bedroom or entire house resembles your thought life? Messy. Cluttered. Unorganized. We may experience the inability to think clearly and communicate with clarity, leaving us feeling overwhelmed and helpless.

We're more likely to respond with anger. As the stress builds inside us throughout our day, our week, our month, it's easy for us to rage at someone or everyone. When stress is at its peak in our lives, we may explode everywhere we go. We can usually recognize people who carry the weight of stress. Their faces reveal anxiety and their tone is sharp and intolerant. Workplaces often cause stress, and stressed people are placed in situations where they need to cooperate with one another or take orders from one another. Tempers, personalities, and stress levels can flare.

We're more likely to sin. Stress can cause us to sin? Absolutely! When we're stressed it's because we're no longer placing our trust and hope in Christ. It also means we aren't keeping our emotional lives in His care. When we have ceased placing our trust in God, we look for other sources and methods to receive peace and calm. The other sources can include alcohol, pornography, food, drugs, excessive online activity, and so forth.

Our emotional and physical health suffers. A growing number of people seem to be experiencing anxiety attacks and other physical manifestations of the deadly emotion of stress. My dear friend Connie, whom I mentioned in the fear chapter, had extreme anxiety attacks because of the tremendous fear she experienced daily. The only thing that saved her was listening to the Word of God on CD every day. Why? Because the Word of God brings healing and is calming to her soul—and ours. Remember, God is our peace.

Become a Life-Giver

God calls us to be peacemakers, to display His glory in all we do. If we are stressed and filled with anxiety, how are we bringing peace to people? How can His glory be revealed through us when we are filled with fear? How are we to give life to people when we are robbed of our joy due to the stresses of life? Give control of your life to God! Allow Him to work in your life in ways you've never imagined or thought possible. Trust in His ways and be at peace, knowing He will work all things for good to those who love him (Romans 8:28).

> Let your light shine before others, so that they may see your good works and give glory to your Father who is in heaven (Matthew 5:16).

The peace Jesus spoke of is the same peace He had when He was hanging on the cross. He knew there was a greater plan in place, knew His Father had all things in control, and knew His suffering was not because His Father wanted to see Him in pain, but that it was for a specific purpose. As followers of Christ we are invited to embrace this same peace, security, and comfort.

This peace is the fruit of our relationship with Christ and from following the principles God set before us in His Word. We are to love, to forgive, to walk in humility, to serve, to not lie, to not steal, to not covet, to not commit adultery, to have no other God's before Him, to honor our parents, to not murder or bear false witness. Following God's will in these areas leads us to peaceful living.

I remember this line from an old song my family used to sing: "I've got peace like a river in my soul." The more we fill ourselves with Christ, the more God's river flows into us and we'll be changed and let His love flow into the lives of those around us.

The Fruit of the Spirit Overcomes Stress

We have talked about how we must exchange our worry for God's peace. How do we walk that out? How do we embrace this fruit of the Spirit and rid ourselves of the stress and worry of everyday living? Jesus is the Prince of Peace. We first must pursue a relationship with Him to receive peace in our lives. From that source of endless and true peace, we are given the strength to pursue relationships in our lives that are born out of love.

> Whoever desires to love life and see good days, let him keep his tongue from evil and his lips from speaking deceit; let him turn away from evil and do good, let him seek peace and pursue it (1 Peter 3:10-11).

God instructs us to seek peace and pursue it. Instead of worrying about something else in your life (like how to overcome stress), think of how to *pursue* peace. Since we've already established from a spiritual perspective that peace comes from our Abba Father, let's address some things that may be hindering our ability to have peace.

1. *Let go of shame, unforgiveness, anger, resentment, bitterness, and guilt*—These are all emotions that create great stress in our lives if they aren't dealt with properly.

2. *Let go of unmet expectations, failures, and disappointments*—We all have dreams, and when those dreams

are not realized it can create tremendous stress and anxiety because we feel out of control. But as believers we have the great advantage of knowing God always has a plan even when we think life looks bleak. He always opens a window when a door is slammed shut. And He always uses the bad, after we repent, for good.

3. *See the good instead of the bad*—Look for the positive in every situation. Be grateful and appreciative for everything. In your relationships focus on the positives.

4. *Evaluate the dead weight in your life*—Think of the unnecessary things in your life causing undue stress. Write them down. Work toward getting rid of those things so you can create a peaceful environment.

5. *World happenings*—If world circumstances create tremendous stress for you, it may be best to not watch every news program on television. Due to today's sensationalism and the graphic nature of TV, be careful what you expose yourself to.

6. *Simplify*—Simplifying our lives tends to brings us peace. The more complicated and cluttered our lives, the harder it is to find our way back to peace. Do you live in a constant state of being overwhelmed? This impacts everything you do and say and think and believe.

In the book *10 Essentials of Highly Healthy People,* Dr. Walt Larimore reports that among the most common emotional troubles that prevent people from becoming highly healthy are stress, anxiety, and depression. He quotes a national survey that states 90 percent of Americans report high levels of stress at least several times a week. Dr. Larimore shares the following physical ailments that are directly related to stress:

- damaged heart and blood vessels
- tense muscles
- suppressed immune system
- hormones released by the body cause the liver to release sugar (for fuel) and at the same time store fat as a backup energy source. But if not used, that fat is deposited—particularly in the abdominal region.
- increased stomach acid that affects the functions of the intestine and colon—leading to gastrointestinal upsets and pain

If we are among the 90 percent, what are we doing to lower our stress level and become healthier?

FREEDOM ACTIONS

1. Surrender your worry to Christ and be anxious for nothing. Simply put, release the outcome to God and leave it in His hands.

2. Exercise regularly; it's been proven that exercise reduces stress. Go for a walk. If you are a mom or your work schedule is hectic and you feel like you can't get out as easily, get a DVD and exercise at home.

3. Maintain a peaceful schedule. Cut out unnecessary errands and activities.

4. Pursue debt-free living.

5. Spend more time without TV, focusing on relationships within the family.

6. Be content in the things you have instead of looking to what you don't have and want.

7. Maintain a peaceful home with peaceful music, lighting, warm decorations, and very little chaos.

8. View your failures as ways to grow and find effective ways to respond to problems so you remain healthy emotionally, spiritually, and physically.

9. Pursue peace in relationships. Toxic relationships can be extremely stressful.

10. Manage your time with structure. We think structure puts us in a box, but it actually frees us. Make out schedules, and keep lists for everything, including a to-do list. This will help to free your mind to focus on peaceful things as opposed to all you have to do.

Freedom Prayer for Stress

Lord, I'm afraid. I'm worried about the daily things of my life. I'm afraid of my financial situation. I'm stressed over my ability to perform at work. And my late-night thoughts are often filled with concerns about my future and getting older. This weight on me is so heavy. I surrender it to You today. I can't carry it. I release the outcome of my life to You. Even if the outcome is not what I expect, I will trust You. Please forgive me for all the times that I haven't trusted You with my life and the lives of those I love. Forgive me for trying to control what I cannot. Today I'm making a change. I'm giving this day, this week, this year, this life… all to You. In Jesus' name. Amen.

For nothing will be impossible with God.

LUKE 1:37

8

The Bondage of Shame

The LORD is merciful and loving, slow to become angry
and full of constant love. He does not keep on rebuking;
he is not angry forever. He does not punish us as we
deserve or repay us according to our sins and wrongs.

PSALM 103:8-10 TEV

In the deepest places of my heart self-hatred resides. I have profound regret for past sin; shame is often worn like a cloak, covering and smothering hope and freedom. I have carried the burden of shame for years because just when I'm making progress, I also seem to hit a reminder of my past—a past I so long to forget. How do we embrace forgiveness of ourselves? To keep ourselves in contempt encourages humility, does it not? Are we to not pay penance for past sin? Our Christian beliefs sometimes get a bit distorted when it comes to shame. We think "self-punishment" instead of forgiveness or in addition to forgiveness—a "just to be sure" measure. If you have struggled with the deadly emotion of shame, it is time to base your understanding on something other than "Pain equals redemption." I have had to walk these steps to overcoming shame, and I want you to know that there truly is freedom on the other side.

The 1986 British film *The Mission* is about a Jesuit priest, Father Gabriel, who enters the South American jungle to build a mission and convert a community of Guarani Indians to Christianity. Rodrigo Mendoza, played by Robert De Niro, is a former unprincipled slave trader and mercenary whose guilty conscience has brought him to the mission to find forgiveness for the sin of murdering his brother. He is so ridden with shame that he denies himself food and clothes himself in sackcloth. As a form of penance he carries his armor, which includes his sword, in a bag over his shoulder through the jungle-ridden mountains of South America.

In one scene he is carrying this heavy, armor-filled bag up a steep mountain. When he arrives at the top, exhausted yet driven by determination, one of the Indians cuts the bag from his back as a symbol of forgiveness. The Indian slave could no longer bare to see Rodrigo carry the burden. Rodrigo thought this physical punishment was necessary to pay for his sin. He needed to *feel* that he had paid for it. Father Gabriel knew Rodrigo was already forgiven, but he let Rodrigo carry the bag because he had to come to the place where he forgave himself. Later on in the film, Rodrigo is so moved by his experience that he devotes himself to the Jesuit mission.

How many of us can relate to Rodrigo Mendoza? Maybe no one but you knows the self-hatred you carry in your bag of sins and transgressions. What is in that heavy bag? The abortion you had as a teenager? The fact that you weren't a virgin when you married? The time you betrayed someone you loved? Maybe your burden of shame is recent, and you are living with the actual sin in motion currently—adultery or an emotional affair or perhaps you're consumed with impure thoughts daily. Maybe your shame relates to thoughts and feelings you've been holding on to that could lead to sinful action—thoughts of committing adultery or leaving your spouse, a desire to see someone else stumble, the temptation to act out of anger or jealousy.

Shame follows many Christians because they have never *felt* like they could be the kind of Christians God wants them to be and calls them to be. They try hard to do everything just right and always fall short. As a result, they never feel loved or accepted by God.

Whatever the case may be, shame is a form of bondage, and God can free us from that bondage. We are not required to pay a penance. Jesus paid it for us; He cut the bags off our backs and carried them for us…to the cross. Just imagine it. We're walking through our lives in total misery, carrying this bag around, and Jesus is next to us saying, "Let it go and give it to Me." Are you ready to be free?

The Root of Shame

At the very root of shame is a sense of self-loathing. A feeling of unforgiveness for the sins of one's past or the sins of someone else we endured. Shame gives the burden-carriers the feeling that something is wrong with them, something is not right with who they are. Shame can come from messages we have told ourselves or even messages others have told us throughout our lives. There is such a thing as "healthy shame": an awareness of conscience telling us that when we sin we should feel ashamed of what we did. But once we repent, the shame should leave us because we have been cleansed by the blood of Christ. The burden has been lifted. Our desire to be martyrs or the lies we continue to believe keep us in bondage when we've really been freed. This is the greatest loss of all. What a waste of the great life we've been given if it is spent in remorse and regret rather than in freedom and in grace.

> Therefore, since we are surrounded by so great a cloud of witnesses, let us also lay aside every weight, and sin which clings so closely, and let us run with endurance the race that is set before us, looking to Jesus, the founder and perfecter of our faith, who for the joy that was set before him endured the cross, despising the shame, and is seated at the right hand of the throne of God (Hebrews 12:1-2).

Why We Experience the Bondage of Shame

How we believe others see us and how we view ourselves is the place where shame can begin. Dale Dunnewold has been counseling for 13 years through Grace Ministries, a counseling center in Nashville that sees hundreds of people a year. Dale shared that shame is one of the strongest deadly emotions he sees people struggle to overcome:

Shame for some people seems to permeate everything they

do. It impacts their ability to relate, to have healthy relationships, and gives them a feeling they are bad in some way.
The root of shame comes down to a message they have told
themselves—that something about them is not okay. They
are dirty or disgusting or maybe they can't even quite put
their finger on what the bad feeling is. It's just something
they feel about themselves.

Dale continued to explain how people act out in their shame and
why shame becomes a familiar friend in some cases.

If I think I'm bad, then I feel rejected by others, and therefore
I put up a wall around my heart and shut people out. Shame
becomes a catalyst for lack of intimacy in relationships. A
friendship relationship and a marriage relationship both
suffer when someone has shame, but what suffers most is the
spiritual relationship. When someone has shame, intimacy
with God is difficult. People think, *I can't hide anything. He
knows it all, so as soon as I open my heart up to Him and expose
who I am, He might reveal to me more things about myself. He
may have me look at my sin, and then I will feel rejected or feel
even worse about who I am. So it's easier to hide and to keep
myself from God.*

A lot of times people with shame say they feel they have intimacy with God. They pray for their family, they pray for God
to give them wisdom in their life, but that is not intimacy
with God. Intimacy with God is saying, "I am going to open
up my heart and let You show me whatever it is You want to
show me. I am going to let You work on the things in my life
that need to change. This is really scary because I don't know
what will happen, but I'm doing it anyway."

God's Truth for the Lies of Shame

You will know the truth, and the truth will set you free (John
8:32).

I asked Dale to share what some of the lies are that people believe when it comes to shame and also the truth he gives them to help in their freedom journey. Together we came up with these lies we tell ourselves, and the truths we need to know to diffuse them.

Lie #1: My problem is too big for God. He could never handle the truth.

The truth: What does the Bible say about our sin and shame? The whole reason Jesus came was to take away our sin and shame. "For He made Him who knew no sin to be sin for us, that we might become the righteousness of God in Him" (2 Corinthians 5:21 NKJV). He took our sin and made us righteous when He died on the cross. So there was this transformation, an exchange that took place on our behalf. God is saying, "I have given you righteousness so you have no more shame." There is no condemnation.

Lie #2: I can't handle what He is going to show me about myself. God won't accept me.

The truth: God accepts us! He loves us! How do we know this? And more importantly, how can we believe this when we are burdened with shameful secrets, a difficult past, the scars of abuse, or the fear of current temptations? There is nothing you can share with God that He does not already know. The opening up of your heart is an act of surrender so that you might have intimacy with Him. God knows everything about you already. He knows the sins you will commit and the sins you have committed, and He accepts you and loves you wholly. His Word is true: "You also, like living stones, are being built into a spiritual house to be a holy priesthood, offering spiritual sacrifices acceptable to God through Jesus Christ. For in Scripture it says: 'See, I lay a stone in Zion, a chosen and precious cornerstone, and the one who trusts in him will never be put to shame'" (1 Peter 2:5-6 NIV).

Lie #3: The messages about me are true—I am so bad and broken that God can't heal me. You might say, "Well, I still feel shame even though I know Christ died and took my shame upon Himself. I just can't stop believing the message."

The truth: The Israelites brought their lambs, sheep, or other animals that could serve as blood sacrifices before God. They would have to come back year after year to rid themselves of sin and shame. Jesus did it once and for all for us, but we must believe it to release the shame.

We need to experience Jesus—experience Him coming into those places where we are broken and refuting the lies we believe about ourselves. Ask yourself what Jesus is saying about the lies you believe. Write down each lie and then pray about it. Ask God to reveal to you the truth about how He sees you to counter how you see yourself. Pray for wisdom and compassion so that you can look at yourself as He does—one worth loving, one worth saving, one worth healing fully.

Lie #4: My deep sin and unrighteousness is too unclean for God and His holiness.

The truth: God is pure, but He can handle our sin. He is righteous, and we are made righteous through His Son, Jesus, who paid the ultimate sacrifice for all sin and all shame. We are made perfect and holy through this covenant with Christ when we accept Him into our hearts. We don't need to be afraid to share anything with Christ. There are many examples in God's Word of believers who failed Him, so we are not alone in our shame and sin: "All have sinned and fall short of the glory of God" (Romans 3:23). On our own and in our own strength and through our human attempts at righteousness we are not worthy, but Jesus has made us clean! He holds us and strengthens us in the ways of God.

We often think what we have done no one else would ever do, and we went too far even by our own standards. We don't accept ourselves, and so we can never be accepted by God. We're just too bad, too horrible for God to fix. These lies keep us in bondage to shame! God accepts us with unconditional love, and He receives us with all our "stuff." He forgives us our past, present, and future sin.

Lie #5: I believe God will be too shocked or too disappointed to take away my shame.

The truth: Dale Dunnewold responds to this lie:

> I see people all the time who come in with important things to share, but they are not sure I can handle it or what my reaction will be. They share a little and see how I respond. If they realize I'm okay with it, they share a little more. We are so afraid we are going to share something and God is going to say, "Oh my gosh! You did that?" That is what shame tells us, that what I feel about myself is true. There is something about me that *is* really bad. What we want more than anything is for someone to say, "I accept you with the problem you have, or the past you have, or the mistakes you've made," but we don't believe it's possible because shame is so strong. Honestly, most people don't accept us unconditionally. As believers they are called to do so, but most don't. We have to be comfortable in what God thinks of us and get to the place where our security is not based on what people think of us, but on what God thinks of us. Our value and acceptance is from God, not man.

> Am I now seeking the approval of man, or of God? Or am I trying to please man? If I were still trying to please man, I would not be a servant of Christ (Galatians 1:10).

Shame Surrendered

We want to believe and embrace freedom in Christ, but the lies are so strong we can't overcome them in our own strength. This is where we need Christ to help us. Thinking positive about our days, our lives, our flaws, our transgressions will not free us from the bondage of shame. Christ and Christ alone gives us victory over our circumstances, when we surrender our will and our shame and guilt in exchange for His gift of a life of freedom and wholeness.

What no eye has seen, nor ear heard, nor the heart of man
imagined, what God has prepared for those who love him
(1 Corinthians 2:9).

When we don't surrender our shame, it shapes our worldview and
our response to those around us. We see our coworkers, friends, and
especially our loved ones from our place of shame. We speak, scold,
accuse, and rant because our shame is too large to contain, and in our
hearts we believe that others have been tainted by our shame or they
also keep such secrets.

Marla's Story

Marla buried the details of her past. She purposely chose to block
them out. What she was unable to shake was the guilt and shame that
came with the experiences she purposely tried to forget. Shame and
guilt were the silent companions she carried with her everywhere. They
never left because of her inability to work through her past. To look at
Marla, you would think that she has everything going for her. She's
beautiful inside and out, successful, very talented, and committed to
being a wonderful wife and mother. What Marla doesn't realize is that
her silent companion of shame, while not evident to those around her,
controls the way she lives out relationships.

Allie is beautiful and on the verge of becoming a young woman.
She is full of curiosity and the excitement of meeting and getting to
know boys. At Allie's age, Marla had already experienced a sexual
relationship. She'd grown up with very different circumstances. By
age five, Marla had already been exposed to alcohol and a mother who
had numerous boyfriends.

The shame Marla carried was the shame she had for her mother
and the shame she had for her own mistakes of sexual sin and promiscuity. Allie never knew of her mother's mistakes, nor did Marla's
husband. Marla kept these secrets safe to preserve the image people
had of her.

One afternoon Marla came home from work and found Allie's

email still up on the screen. Unable to resist the temptation to read it, Marla skimmed the private exchange and was alarmed to find that Allie had been emailing back and forth with a boy from school—and it was very personal. Marla reacted. She screamed at Allie and spoke words to shame her, to make her feel as degraded as if she had slept with this boy rather than just communicated with him.

Marla also often shamed her husband any time *she felt* he was somehow betraying her trust.

By making Allie and her husband feel ashamed, Marla was letting her unchecked deadly emotion destroy her daughter's innocence and her husband's trust. Marla had a choice to make—seek healing in her life and for her relationships or possibly drive Allie to the very things she feared and alienating her husband.

Deadly Consequences of Shame

I spent years in bondage to shame, thinking if I hung on to it, somehow it would keep me in a place of humility. What it did was keep me in a place of ineffectiveness for Christ. I did not and could not see myself with the authority God gave me, the authority to walk in all He has purposed for my life. I didn't feel good enough, worthy enough, perfect enough. Anytime God called me to something, I was reluctant or unwilling. I thought that there were others who were much more qualified for the position or task.

People could tell me that I was smart, beautiful, qualified, and pre-pared, but it didn't penetrate the shame. I could achieve great success and still the shame lingered. It wasn't until I allowed God to open up those places of guilt and shame that healing began. The more I have permitted God to work on my heart, to heal my heart, to come into those places and reverse the lies I believed for so long, the more I have experienced freedom.

To get beyond my self-contempt and self-hatred, I had to take steps to forgive myself. Here are the deadly consequences of shame and the steps required to counter, work through, and see beyond each consequence.

Lack of self-acceptance or sense of value. I had to accept myself in the place I was in when I felt ashamed. Whether I was sinning or someone shamed me, I had to accept the situation and know it was not God's heart to see me hurt or see me in my sin. He grieved yet He still loved me.

Disobedience. I had to obey. I heard a sermon once that really changed the way I looked at myself when it came to forgiving me. The pastor commented that it is a sin not to forgive ourselves just like it is sin not to forgive others. It distracts us from God when we are focused on ourselves and what we have done; therefore, it keeps us from God's best and His direction. We'll miss the mark over and over in our pursuit of godliness and righteousness if we are obsessed with our own actions.

Quick judgment of others and ourselves. I had to learn to extend to myself the same mercy I extended to others and the same mercy God extends to me. This was not easy. I had to look at myself as if I were looking at someone else completely. Like the person I used to be was not me, but a friend. How would I treat a friend who had endured the same wounded past I endured? This helped me have mercy for myself and made me realize the harshness with which I treated myself. How would you treat yourself as a friend? Would you have compassion and mercy? Would you offer patience and a safe place to open up?

Imprisoned and unable to move forward. If you are frozen in life, it is no surprise. Shame can build up walls faster and higher than any other deadly emotion. I learned to survive through the pain I came through by forming walls of self-protection. I had to become comfortable with being uncomfortable before I could experience a breakthrough because I needed to just "be" and to see these walls for what they were—barriers between me and full living. I also came to realize that the more I pursued Christ in my life, the more the shame diminished. The deeper in love I become with Him, the more I grasp how much He loves me as His daughter.

A distorted view of self. When we live with shame, we hold on to a view of ourselves that is not the view God has of us. He sees us with eyes of love and adoration, and we believe God sees us with appalling rejection. Ask the Lord to help you see yourself through His eyes, how He really sees you. When thoughts about yourself come into your mind, focus on God's adoration for you.

What is keeping you from your pursuit of freedom? What do you fear most about opening up your heart? Are you afraid God will not love you? Are you afraid looking at the past will put you back there again? I can tell you, my friend, pursue freedom. It is worth the amount of work it takes. It is worth facing the past and opening up old wounds. They will not overtake you. God will help you walk through them, and you will finally be free from the lies you have believed for so long. Lies like "You are not good enough, not loved enough, not godly enough." As long as shame is a close friend, it will keep you from having healthy relationships and negatively impact the way you view yourself and others. Emotional wholeness awaits you in Christ!

Become a Life-Giver

> To you, O LORD, I lift up my soul. O my God, in you I trust; let me not be put to shame; let not my enemies exult over me (Psalm 25:1-2).

Shame robs us of our ability to give life. It distracts us, causing us to be focused on ourselves instead of others. As we continue to move toward wholeness, people will see a quiet confidence in us due to the peace of Christ permeating our being. Peace brings us a sense of authority that draws people toward us, instead of repelling people due to insecurity and neediness.

When we have shame, we struggle with looking into people's eyes because we don't feel worthy. We suffer from insecurity and trust issues. We cover up our weaknesses and create an image of who we want people to see, which creates a false sense of intimacy. When we are embracing healing in our lives, we are able to share healing truth with others. When we overcome and can share Christ glorified in our lives, people will listen and take heart. It helps them move toward their freedom. Hurting people hurt others, and healed people help heal others. Press in and fight for your healing. You have to want it. You have to want to be transformed forever.

The Fruit of the Spirit Overcomes Shame

> Let your gentleness be evident to all. The Lord is near. Do not be anxious about anything, but in everything, by prayer and petition, with thanksgiving, present your requests to God. And the peace of God, which transcends all understanding, will guard your hearts and your minds in Christ Jesus (Philippians 4:5-7 NIV).

Shame is a very harsh, deadly emotion. It eats away at us spiritually and emotionally. I believe that over time it also manifests physically as it dictates our actions and interactions. But we can seek gentleness, the fruit of the Spirit that helps us overcome our shame. When deep shame is experienced, it is easier to beat ourselves up over and over than seek refuge in God's gentleness because we feel unworthy. But the attraction of kindness, compassion, and the sweetness of God's grace is enough to bring us to gentleness. In God we find refreshment for our souls and refuge for our broken hearts. He soothes the pain of even the most difficult trials and dulls the edges of our indiscretions.

Gentleness is a reminder of the comfort we find in Christ and in our complete salvation in Him. Let the Shepherd lead you out of shame and into safety and healing with His gentle grace.

FREEDOM ACTIONS

1. *Trust your advocate.* Whether people have made you feel ashamed, you feel ashamed because you've never fit in, or you feel your past guilt has driven you to shame, remember you have an advocate in

Christ. He is on your side and in your court. He will restore what has been lost and repair what has been destroyed. Memorize this scripture and bring it to mind when shame visits you: "My little children, I am writing these things to you so that you may not sin. But if anyone does sin, we have an advocate with the Father, Jesus Christ the righteous" (1 John 2:1).

2. *Forgive yourself.* I remember the first time God really dealt with me on forgiving myself. I was working a job that allowed me a lot of freedom to pray and read my Bible. One afternoon I turned the radio on, and the host began to discuss abortion. Before I knew it, I was sobbing uncontrollably. I realized at that moment I still needed healing for the abortion I had taken part in six years earlier. I thought when I got saved that was enough. I thought I had been healed when I asked forgiveness, but in that moment I knew my pain was deeper than just a quick moment of healing. While praying, I felt God gently urging me to write on a piece of paper, "I forgive the girl of my past" over and over again. I started to write. It was hard. I didn't want to forgive that girl. I didn't want to release her from her iniquity. But as I wrote out each line over and over, tears streaming down my face, God began to give me eyes to see her. To see her pain, her lost soul. I began to forgive. Take a moment and write out over and over, "I forgive the girl of my past." If you were an adult when you sinned, write out, "I forgive the woman of my past."

3. *Stop performing and start praising.* When we live in shame we feel we aren't good enough for God. We believe the falsehood that we have to "earn" our right to the kingdom. We are not saved by works, but by grace alone. There is nothing we can do to earn our salvation. It is already paid for and bought by Jesus on the cross. So you are free. No more performing and trying to be perfect. It is out of our passion, our love for Christ, that we desire to do things for God. Like a wife to her husband, we long to do for Him because

we adore Him, we love Him so much we want to take care of His needs. As we abide in Him, and He in us, we desire to be obedient to His Word.

4. *Reflect for a moment.* Write down the places of shame and guilt in your life. Now, what are the lies associated with your sin? Take a moment and pray over each incident. Ask Jesus to speak to your heart about each circumstance, each pain, each point of guilt. Feel the embrace of God's grace. Don't focus on the list of things you should have done and didn't. Only use the list to submit each bit of shame to God's hands.

> The Lord GOD will help Me;
> Therefore I will not be disgraced;
> Therefore I have set My face like a flint,
> And I know that I will not be ashamed.
> He is near who justifies Me;
> Who will contend with Me?
> Let us stand together.
> Who is My adversary?
> Let him come near Me (Isaiah 50:7 NKJV).

Freedom Prayer for Shame

Lord, I have hated myself for so long. I need Your help to forgive me, to forgive my past. Heal my heart. Help me not to shame others because of the sin and shame in my own life. Open my eyes to what You want to show me. Open my ears to what You want me to hear from You. Help me, Lord, to surrender the pain and sorrow I've endured. Help me surrender my temptation to hang on to this shame as a way to pay penance for my sin. Deliver me and forgive me for allowing this shame and unforgiveness to remain in my life. In Jesus' name. Amen.

9

The Loneliness of Pride

Be submissive to those who are older. All of you, clothe
yourselves with humility toward one another, because,
"God opposes the proud but gives grace to the humble."

1 PETER 5:5 NIV

Mark sat quietly as the judge announced his sentence. He was familiar with the courthouse process because it wasn't the first time he had been there. "One year of community service, one year of anger management," the judge announced with a solemn tone. Mark grimaced slightly. His lawyer was just glad Mark was not going to have to do jail time. As they left the courtroom Mark turned to his lawyer and said in an angry manner, "I shouldn't have to do anger management or community service. This is all 'her' fault, and I know she is in cahoots with the judge or something!" The "her" Mark was speaking of was his fourth wife. She'd pressed charges against him for assault, just as his other three wives had.

In the beginning Mark seemed charming and handsome enough. He had grown up in a wonderful Christian home and went to church every weekend. But his pride was keeping him from cultivating healthy relationships. He refused to admit he was wrong or sorry about anything. No matter how many people, counselors, friends, and family members would tell him to look at his negative behaviors and sinful actions, he refused to do it. How could he have a teachable spirit when a teachable spirit is birthed out of humility? Being humble was not a discipline he practiced. He preferred to shift blame. By his fourth marriage, he should have at least begun to wonder if something might need to be looked at in his life, but not Mark. Instead he lived the rest of his life alone, drifting in and out of relationships with no commitment. It was a much easier route than having to admit something needed to change.

> *According to Christian teachers, the essential vice, the utmost*
> *evil, is Pride. Unchastity, anger, greed, drunkenness, and*
> *all that, are mere flea bites in comparison: it was through*
> *Pride that the devil became the devil: Pride leads to every*
> *other vice: it is the complete anti-God state of mind.*
>
> C.S. Lewis, *Mere Christianity*

Lewis went on to say, "Pride gets no pleasure out of having something, only out of having more of it than the next man." How easy it is for us to take pride in the performance of our Christianity or the posturing and posing we emulate in our Christian walk. Such effort is taken so that good comments point back to us about how great "we" look and how well "we" do. What is our faith about? The way we are perceived or having a heart after God's own? Lewis said, "Pride is spiritual cancer: it eats up the very possibility of love, or contentment, or even common sense." Mark's opportunity for true love was lost over and over again because of his refusal to admit his problems and work through them. He let the cancer spread.

The Root of Pride

I saved pride for last because it is a catalyst for the other deadly emotions. Pride says, "I am greater than God. I have more knowledge than God." The root of pride is enmity toward God. Even if our pride doesn't seem like an expression of hostility toward the Lord, it becomes a constant barrier between us and Him...and between us and others.

Pride seeks to win. It says, "I am better than you," and invites competition in relationships. Humility desires others to succeed and recognizes our frailty and inadequacies, as well as our need for God.

Pride is about positioning—positioning ourselves to be richer than the richest, smarter than the smartest, better looking than the best looking, never satisfied with where we are at, always wanting more and needing more in order to feel secure. But the only security that can emerge from pride is a counterfeit sense in ourselves.

No one wants to admit to being prideful. We might act out of a prideful heart, but we don't often recognize that we are leaning on and lifting up ourselves rather than God. There is such a trend toward positive thinking, which can be very helpful and healing for a person who has dwelled on fear or negative experiences. But positive thoughts should not be given more power than they have. They are not God's will; they are frequently only about our own. They do not replace faith and trust in our Creator. And for some, they usher in the view that we are able to be our own gods. As gods our focus becomes quick success, monetary gain, or the accolades of others. The idea of God being a big Santa appeals to our prideful nature. There is part of us that wants to take over for Him in our own lives. No? Think about how often you try to take charge of your family's well-being, your career, your relationships, and so forth.

The person who believes in the power of thoughts instead of the power of God's will eventually loses sight of God's priorities: providing for family, meeting the needs of the community and the church, serving God, and serving our purpose in God. Greed can lure many believers into the church of positive thinking. The world tells us that there is another way to pray and play. It sounds so appealing because it is based on the "works" idea. If "I" do this, "I" can earn the right to have the greatest the world has to offer.

Why Pride Emerges

Remember the disciples of Christ asking, "Who is the greatest in the kingdom of heaven?" (Matthew 18:1 NIV). Jesus tells them (and us) they must become as a little child to even enter the kingdom of heaven, and a person must humble himself as a little child to be the greatest. Children are dependent completely on others for their resources and for their existence. They have not rooted themselves in accomplishments or titles. They have no inhibition to love and be loved. They have not mastered the posturing and positioning to get ahead, to be one up on the rest of the world.

This is opposite of what our culture feeds us. Culture tells us that to become great we must exalt ourselves, we must fight our way to the top, we must rely on our own resources because no one will help us get there. Self-preservation then sets in, and pride quickly follows.

A friend of mine lost an executive position with a major ministry because of his desire to win, manifested by his overriding the organization's procedures with his own opinion, will, and goals. He felt his way of doing things was more ethical, more practical, and just plain better. The desire to see things change was not wrong, but his approach, attitude, and prideful pursuit were wrong, and they cost him his job. His pride reared itself in a way that offended the company leaders, and they let him go.

There is a fine line between being arrogant and exerting wisdom. The two approaches make all the difference in the way people receive things. And they reflect different hearts. One of my kids had quite a time in school. Basically he just didn't like it. I had a lot of interaction with the school officials and his teachers. One of his teachers came across as very arrogant. She couldn't be corrected and seemed annoyed when I asked her questions regarding my son. I felt very intimidated by her and knew why my son was struggling with the same issue. The school authorities corrected her in one of our meetings, which softened her some, but she remained negative. I told my son he was going to have to work with her and understand there will always be people in his life he doesn't necessarily care for or connect with. We spent too much time in the principal's office that year, but there was progress, and we even grew to like this teacher, despite the lack of change on her part.

The following year my son had a teacher who will likely go down in history as one of the best teachers he ever had. He flourished under her leadership. She still corrected him, but she exerted her wisdom with gentleness and kindness, not with a prideful arrogance that fueled his own pride and resistance.

> When pride comes, then comes disgrace, but with the humble
> is wisdom (Proverbs 11:2).

A prideful stance tends to inspire pride in others. That isn't exactly a characteristic we want to bring out in the people we live with or work with or minister to. Wisdom exerted with kindness and love is like a perfectly good cup of hot tea. Any hotter, and it would be impossible to drink, too cold and its flavor diminishes. But just the right temperature and sweetness and the tea is wonderful. You can have all the wisdom in the world, but if you approach people in a way that is received as arrogant, your message—no matter how important—will not be received. Or you can approach people with a humility that says, "I am teachable. I am willing to hear what you think as I also share what I know."

In my friend's case, if he had let go of his determination to prove his findings and his rightness, and instead led with gentleness and openness, people most likely would have eventually come to him and asked him his thoughts. He had the position in the company—the authority—but the best approach was not there because of his pride. In my son's situation, it was the teacher who had tremendous wisdom and patience who impacted him the most, and we're still seeing the results today.

When we are kind, when we exert our wisdom with great humility, we are able to achieve so much more. When we don't demand or exert a sense of entitlement that comes from a prideful position of posturing, we are able, in most cases, to achieve much, and what a great witness we are as disciples of Christ.

How do you treat people when you interact with them day to day? As a follower of Christ, what impression do you want to leave with people? Do you want to always win or do you want to help build up the body of Christ?

I'll never forget sitting down with a prominent senior pastor of a large church. I held him in high esteem. He said to me when asked a theological question, "I don't know." I was amazed at his honesty and willingness to admit that he didn't know the answer. He not only admitted to not knowing, he then went on to ask me my thoughts about the topic, which furthered my respect for him as a leader. Am I willing to be this kind of leader? A leader who admits not knowing something to someone who holds me in high esteem? I hope so! But think about how easy it is to pretend we know the answers even when we don't to save face and not look foolish. In those moments, our inclination toward pride is tested.

> And he who does not take his cross and follow after Me is not worthy of Me (Matthew 10:38 NKJV).

Are we like the little children Jesus spoke of? Do we rely on God completely for our resources, our existence? Have we given Him the glory for everything in our lives?

A King Dethroned

King Saul was the first king to the Israelites. In physical form he was extraordinary—a head taller than the rest of the tribe. He was chosen by God to deliver the Israelites from the hands of their enemies, but early on Saul showed signs of disobedience and disregard for the Lord's commands. God's disappointment in Saul is expressed through the prophet Samuel, who tells Saul he will no longer reign as king, and God will begin searching for a man after His own heart, a man who will obey the Lord instead of taking matters into his own hands. Saul's pride continues to be evident as he reigns with irreverence to the Lord, making sacrifices apart from God's commandments, taking plunder from the enemies of Israel when he knew this was defiance to God, and shifting blame to the people for his mistakes. Saul is rebuked harshly by God through Samuel, "For rebellion is as the sin of witchcraft, and stubbornness is as iniquity and idolatry. Because you have rejected the word of the LORD, He also has rejected you from being king" (1 Samuel 15:23 NKJV).

God makes it more than evident he despises pride, but most important, He despises the outcome of pride, which is disobedience. Saul continued to ignore the directions and requirements God gave him through Samuel.

How many times have we ignored God's Word and instruction? We may not have a prophet who comes to us and gives us the layout for our Christian journey, but we have God's Word. We have example after example of the way we should and should not walk out our life with God. God always provided a vision for what He wanted the people to do, what He wanted the people to even say at times, and how He wanted them to live. He pointed them in the way they should go. God points us to His Word to direct our paths and give us wisdom in the ways we should go. Are we so prideful we won't listen? Will we continue to do things our way, lean on our own understanding? Are we so prideful we won't be obedient to His Word out of our love for Him?

Saul did not revere God or he would have obeyed God. Do we revere God or do we let Him in our lives occasionally…when we feel we "need" Him to come through for us? Do we have a personal relationship with Him or is our journey with Him more about a bunch of rules set before us and a life of obligation? The Bible is a literal story that reveals the very nature of God and Jesus Christ. This story is meant to inspire us to run the race of life with great perseverance because we see the prize God has set before us. He has given us His vision.

What happens when we go our own way as Saul did? When we refuse to listen, refuse to obey, refuse to change? When we refuse to honor God in all we do?

Who Do We Want People to See?

When I was getting ready to speak one night, I felt the Lord saying, "Michelle, I want you to share about your abortion." I had kept this secret for so many years and was very ashamed. I had no desire for people to know about it. I really enjoyed that people saw me as a "woman of God" who had it together. After living a life of rebellion as a teenager, it felt good to have the respect of others and have them see me as a model wife and mother. I was reluctant to share the abortion information for fear of rejection and because I wanted to look good to people.

It was my pride that kept me from wanting to share with women this place of shame in my life. I argued with God and told Him I couldn't share it. I asked, "Why? Why do You want me to share this, Lord?" Then the Lord really spoke to me with a life-changing message: "Michelle, who do you want people to see? Do you want people to see Me, or do you want people to see you? Do you want Me to be glorified in your testimony, or do you want to be glorified?"

It was a moment of awakening that has stuck with me all these years, and I remember it every time I speak. I am only transparent because of the word the Lord gave me that night. It was not an easy word to get. I was scared to follow through, but knew that I needed to put my image aside in order to shed light on the Redeemer. As I shared with women that evening, I felt confident the Lord would go before me and soften their hearts to hear my message. If God was for me, who could be against me?

When God calls you to a place of obedience, He will cover you and give you strength to see it through. I was astonished at the number of women who approached me afterward to share their experiences of abortions and how hearing my story of forgiveness and freedom helped them get free from their guilt and shame. Everything to God's glory!

Deadly Consequences of Pride

When pride rules over us, controls us, it cuts us off from spiritual growth and maturity. We no longer hear God. Just like Saul, our hearts are hardened and we lean on our own understanding instead of His Word. So what are some of the deadly consequences?

We are in enmity with God when we're filled with pride. When we are prideful, we are self-serving. We become consumed with building our treasures up, our kingdom up—not building God's treasures up in heaven and expanding His kingdom.

Destruction is evident. God speaks clearly in His Word regarding pride as it related to destruction for individuals and for nations. He speaks to the pride in the hearts of Israel as a nation (Hosea 7:10), and He speaks to us personally on what pride will reap in our lives: "Pride goes before destruction, a haughty spirit before a fall" (Proverbs 16:18 NIV).

Its roots are handed down through generations. I picked up a book the other day about the generational pride that had been handed down in a family. Hardened hearts and arrogance kept this family in bondage for generations. This sinful legacy led to murder, affairs, jealousy, greed, division, and more. Finally, after years of pride, two brothers' hearts were changed and moved toward obedience to Christ. They not only changed, but they reversed the cancer of pride that had been in their family for years. No longer would their children be raised with hate and evil in their hearts. They would be raised with love and compassion for the needs of others. No longer would selfish ambition and gain be the preached priority in life.

If we are prideful and decide to cut off God's leading and wisdom even in the smallest way, we are planting roots that will grow stronger for each generation. We emulate what we see, and if children see pride, they will copy it and teach that nature unless God transforms them individually and shows them their sin. Anger, hate, selfish behavior, greed, self-righteousness, lack of common sense, jealousy, fear, shame, stress, confusion, division, unhealthy competition, bitterness, and unforgiveness are the fruit of pride.

Lack of contentment. Ultimately we are horribly insecure because our foundation is based on self-fulfillment, achievement, and success— all empty pursuits that leave us longing for more of something. We are unable to enjoy the simple things because simple is not something we can be proud of. We are obsessed with posturing and looking good on the outside. This breeds lack of contentment and spawns self-righteousness and a religious spirit that kills and destroys.

God's Truth for the Lies of Pride

Lie #1: A positive outlook is the same as faith. We're surrounded by messages of positive thinking. That we can change our lives through our thoughts and in our own power is a constant message in today's world.

The truth: A positive outlook is part of faith, but it's never a replacement for faith. We are to train our thoughts on the things of God, and from this, we grow in spiritual and emotional health. We become more content and fulfilled. Pride and our sense of independence make us want to take control of our fate and future by assuming we have the power to do so by merely thinking it into being.

> Do not conform any longer to the pattern of this world, but be transformed by the renewing of your mind. Then you will be able to test and approve what God's will is—his good, pleasing and perfect will (Romans 12:2 NIV).

Lie #2: We can love God and make worldly success a priority.

The truth: Your rise up the corporate ladder or into a bigger house is not a spiritual pursuit. You can pray about these things, and they can be very important in your life. They might even be part of God's blessings in your life. But if these or other pursuits—from golden opportunities to retiring in style—are your focus, your spirit will not be centered on the choices and directions God wants you to make and take. And you don't want to miss God's version of success that is designed just for you.

> No one can serve two masters, for either he will hate the one and love the other, or he will be devoted to the one and despise the other. You cannot serve God and money (Matthew 6:24).

Lie #3: We have more to offer others than they have to offer us. Prideful people only hear themselves. They don't hear correction and are not teachable. They are unable to grow.

The truth: We have a lot to learn from others, and often they are introduced to our lives for a very good reason—maybe even to help us work on some of our deadly emotions. If you find it difficult to partner with people, consider why that is. Make efforts toward community and connection. Become your best by hearing the many other voices, ideas, and opinions of your coworkers, your family members, and the body of Christ.

Lie #4: Our winning and achieving makes God look good.

The truth: If we first seek glory so we can pass it along to God, we have our priorities switched. It is true that if you experience success and achieve areas of influence, crediting God can lead others to praise Him. But keeping your eye on the prize should mean that you are keeping your heart on Jesus and His desires for your life—not on a particular level of world status or success. God doesn't need us to make Him look good. He is good. And when we push our pride aside and let His goodness flow through us and change us inside out, our praises are sincere, powerful, and true.

> Where your treasure is, there your heart will be also (Matthew 6:21).

Become a Life-Giver

When we are filled with pride, or even struggle with pride, it is almost impossible to give life to others. Instead, our focus is getting or taking from others. When deadly pride enters our lives, we are reluctant to praise others or give them credit and encouragement because we don't want to turn attention away from us. Some people may even take attention away from others by claiming credit for what they've done or offering self-praise instead of commenting on another's participation. Do you see how this tears down that person and yourself? What feels like the glow of recognition may really be the heat of disapproval from others if they sense arrogance and reluctance to be humble and kind.

Pride leads us to want more power, more success, more of everything. We rob others of the joy of success because we must be more successful. We rob them of the confidence of achievement or accomplishment because we must accomplish or achieve more than they do. We rob them of self-esteem because we must be better than they are. Do we take joy in other people's successes? Do we help people in ways that help them grow and achieve more? Are we okay with letting others take the limelight? Pride is a very subtle deadly emotion because it makes us arrogant, which makes us blind and deaf to those around us.

The Fruit of the Spirit Overcomes Pride

Linda was driving to lunch and the two-lane road was merging into one lane. The car beside her began to speed up to pass her. As they did, Linda blurted out to herself with her kids watching and listening closely, "They are not going to pass me. I'll show them who will win." Determined to not let the other car get in front of her, Linda also sped up. The other car sped up again. Linda sped up some more. Finally the driver of the other car slowed down and moved in behind Linda, but Linda almost succeeded in running the other car off the road due to her desire to win and show who was boss. If Linda had approached the merging traffic with a particular fruit of the spirit, her pride wouldn't have had a chance to take over. That fruit is kindness, and it directs our hearts, actions, thoughts, and attention to others.

We are not in the equation when we extend kindness. We are serving God by serving others. We are showing God's grace when we are forgiving another. We are manifesting God's goodness when we offer help to a stranger. We are walking God's truth when we encourage others and help them along their paths. We are portraying God's faithfulness when we follow through for our families and others, especially when it involves sacrifice on our part. Kindness removes the "I" of our situation and allows the focus to be about God and others.

Yes, we are part of the situation because we're being obedient and our paths and purposes greatly matter to God. But we are not serving ourselves. The limelight is on the giver (God) and on the receiver (the other person).

We aren't perfect, and we find ourselves taking part in prideful actions every day. We fume at people in grocery lines who are slow. We get angry with people on the road because we feel we have the right to control things. We take on a sense of ownership and authority when we are at a restaurant ordering the wait staff around. We generally have a sense of entitlement about life. We aren't evil people, but we are broken and in need of God's heart for others. It is easy to write this off by thinking, *I'm not* that *bad*. But ask yourself if you honestly put God and others before yourself. Do you pull back from building up a relationship because you don't want to sacrifice your pursuits or pleasures? Do you raise your hand in self-righteous anger when you don't get your way?

Are we humble as Christ taught us to be? Kindness is born out of love, and if we have no love we are virtually nothing. Where is the love? It begins with a relationship with Christ and an understanding of true humility.

FREEDOM ACTIONS

1. *Don't shift blame.* When you are faced with a situation where you're at fault, don't shift the blame. Take responsibility. Even if you feel you're not at fault, be open to hear what your accusers are saying, and be willing to change or adjust accordingly. Give and go the extra mile in relationships. There are times when it may be necessary to hear people's grievances against you, and while you may not understand them, you can ask God to give you eyes to see the situation from their perspective in order for you to reconcile.

2. *Remove the idols.* If wealth is an idol, if your job is an idol, if your large house is your idol, if your appearance is an idol…pray about

removing the position these things have in your heart. Ask God to show you how to remove them from being your focus. Anything that is causing you to have pride needs to be removed from the position of being an idol in your heart. We tend to think of the big things, such as wealth and career, as the main idols for people, but when you examine your life, you may be surprised to find that it is often the lesser things that we obsess over, spend our money on, and give our time to.

3. *Be teachable and pliable.* When we are controlled by pride, we are unteachable and inflexible. We are resistant to change because we feel in control of everything. God isn't able to move and we aren't able to grow when we're not open to the changes He wants to make in our lives. When we're not open to being taught by others, when we're not pliable, we miss out on the direction God has for us. And God's purpose for us is greatly hindered. Wisdom tells us to approach people in humility, not with prideful arrogance that says we're better than they are. Greet people with a genuine desire to learn from them, not with a desire to teach them what you know.

4. *Get rid of the entitlement mentality.* The older I get the more I realize life is so not about me. It is about everyone but me. This is the Christian journey. Even my purpose is not about me! It's about Christ, who lives in me. Instead of approaching life always thinking about what you are going to get (which is completely saying life is all about me), approach life with "What can I give." Go to church in the same way. We tend to evaluate church by what we are getting from it instead of thinking, *What can I contribute to this body of people, this church building, the children who represent the next generation of believers?* In giving, we are humbled by how much we learn from the experiences.

5. *Be an obedient listener.* Prideful people don't enjoy listening to others. They want to hear themselves talk, hear themselves give

advice. Begin to listen to others. It is amazing what you will receive in doing so. Hearing the stories of others will also help you appreciate what you have.

Remember Saul? He was so prideful he didn't listen and obey God. His disobedience was so abhorrent that the Lord cut off his kingdom. God looks at our hearts, and we know when we are choosing our way over God's way. Obedience to God's Word and to His promptings in our lives is essential to living a life of humility. Humbleness gives honor to God and removes the idol of self from our being.

6. *Give life and be a good model for the next generation.* Stop the curse of pride from being handed down in your family. It can end with you if you will humble yourself before God and repent.

7. *Embrace love and kindness; toss out greed and malice.* Put others before you and allow God to handle the outcome of the persistence of your enemies. Think on ways to *give life* instead of robbing people of their joy.

8. *Be content in all things.* Paul reminds us in Philippians of his contentment: "I know how to be brought low, and I know how to abound. In any and every circumstance, I have learned the secret of facing plenty and hunger, abundance and need. I can do all things through [Christ] who strengthens me" (Philippians 4:12-13). Like Paul, we also need to be content in all things. Whether we have plenty or nothing at all, Christ abounds, and He is with us always. He is enough for us.

Freedom Prayer for Pride

Lord, forgive me for having pride. Help me see the areas in which I am prideful. Shed Your light on every corner of my heart that is not submitted to You wholly. Teach me what genuine humility is. Reveal to me areas of disobedience that are a result of pride in my life, and give me the wisdom to communicate in love and not arrogance. Lord, give me the desire to serve others instead of myself. Give me a kindness that overflows for friends, family, strangers...all Your children. Thank You for giving me strength to walk out these principles in my life. In Jesus' name. Amen.

*Your faith should not be in the wisdom of
men but in the power of God.*

1 CORINTHIANS 2:5 NKJV

10

The Power to Be Free from Deadly Emotions

*Work designed for eternity can only be done
by the eternal spirit.*

A.W. TOZER

Anna had grown up in a church-going family and had heard about God, but she never had a real relationship with Christ until she was in her mid-twenties. She'd been sexually abused as a child by her uncle from the time she was three until she was in her late teens. He was finally convicted and sent away for sexually abusing another child. Anna was set free physically from his hands of torture, but spiritually, mentally, and emotionally was a whole different matter. After accepting Christ into her heart, she felt the forgiveness she'd always longed for and thought her new life in Christ would mean an end to her pain. But it didn't.

Anna went on to become a very successful businesswoman, married a wonderful Christian man, and had a couple of children, and yet her past still haunted her. She couldn't forget the sexual abuse and felt it defined her. No matter what she did, no matter how much success she attained, she never felt free. Anna began to medicate the emotions with alcohol so that she could feel a sense of peace and calm, but it would only ease the pain temporarily and it enhanced her feelings of shame. She had a secret life of fear, shame, guilt, and unforgiveness, and now she could go ahead and add "hypocrite" because of her inability to live the Christian life in a way God and others expected her to.

In her mind she knew the right answers. She was set free when she came to Christ. So why did she not feel free? Why did she continue to slip in and out of unhealthy, secretive behavior? As her kids got older and some of the stresses in marriage began to materialize, she felt things falling apart. When she would meet with people she would wonder, *Do they know my past? Do they know the horrible shame I carry? The horrible anguish in my soul because of the pain I endured? Do they know the anger I have because I felt violated and unprotected by my mother and father?* She didn't think anyone would understand. She hadn't even told her husband. She was too embarrassed and felt responsible for what had happened.

As Anna's inner turmoil increased, her feeling of anguish did as well. She finally realized this was beyond her ability to control, and she knew she had to get help. She recognized that she couldn't continue to wear a mask and hide her past from everyone. At the recommendation of a friend, Anna found a counselor. As the counselor began to ask Anna questions and explore the areas of pain, Anna would feel physically ill. Her stomach would churn and her body would break out in a cold sweat. She felt like she was suffocating. She wasn't prepared to allow the counselor to open up this box of deadly emotions. Her anguish, her bitterness, was deeply rooted. She had closed off a part of her spirit and felt emotionally unable to open it back up.

The counselor graciously assured her this was going to be a long process and for her to not feel threatened or discouraged if she wasn't able to willingly share right away. He let her know there were no expectations, and he was there to help her, not further hurt her.

Anna knew she could never have a future, a life of freedom, until she faced these demons of her past. She mightily pursued the freedom she so desired, but it took years of breaking through the bondage of the lies she had so long believed. Once her freedom slowly became apparent, peace and emotional wholeness permeated her being. Most important, she had opened her heart back up to God. Shame was not controlling her, fear was not controlling her, lust was not controlling her, pride was not controlling her, jealousy was not controlling her, anger was not controlling her, and she was no longer filled with stress and anxiety. Sure, the emotions would visit her and those lies would haunt her now and then, but she recognized them immediately and was able to dismiss them for what they were—lies from the enemy of her soul.

What is controlling you? Is it jealousy? Is it fear, anger, pride, lust, or stress? Is your shame keeping you from confidence to pursue your purpose? God wants us to be free by overcoming these deadly emotions with His truths and His strength. God gave us His Word so we would have the answers to questions and concerns while on our quest for freedom.

When the Israelites were in bondage to Pharaoh, their hearts cried out in despair. They desperately called out to God to save them from the controlling hand of Pharaoh. They became so beaten down by their enslavement and so anguished in their spirit they really had lost all hope. Have you lost hope? Have you closed off your spirit to the point you can no longer hear freedom calling you? Can you no longer discern truth due to cruel bondage? Ask God to open your heart again so you can experience the true freedom He so longs to give you.

> *The cure...for every form of slavery to something other than God is worship. Not the dull worship of rote routine, or the worship of contrived excitement, but worship that creates deep pleasure in the One who receives it, and the one who gives it. Only a thrill-seeking, soul-pleasuring encounter with God that generates more pleasure than sin will free us from our addiction to sin.*
>
> Larry Crabb

It is the quest for growing in Christ and experiencing the continued filling of the Holy Spirit in our lives that frees us and gives us the strength to overcome.

Finding the Power to Overcome Deadly Emotion

Over Christmas break I was sitting in front of the fire talking with some friends. One of them said to me, "Michelle, do you know what it takes for a fire to be great?" I thought back to memories of my dad building a fire in our fireplace and remembered him pulling pages from the local paper. I blurted out, "Newspapers!" He politely laughed and went on to tell me the story he wanted me to hear in the first place. He said that a great fire requires two important components. The hot fiery coals are the foundation for the fire, but the fire is fanned by the flow of air moving through it.

The flame of faith requires the same two important components: Jesus is the firm foundation (the hot coals) in our lives; the Holy Spirit (the wind) is what God uses to fuel and build the work accomplished by His Son on the cross. The hot coals and the rush of air together keep the wood ablaze. The Holy Spirit fans the flame of Christ in our lives, and when we surrender ourselves to the Spirit, our hearts light up with passion and faithfulness and longing to live God's Word. But when we persist in controlling our lives in the flesh, we grieve the Holy Spirit by limiting the flame and the potential for a full-blaze faith.

The world implores us to resort to human efforts, common sense, posturing, and positioning ourselves for great success, propping ourselves up for self-worship. But the Spirit calls us to the ways of God, the wisdom of His Word, the positioning of His reign in our lives, and to a walk of humility and surrender.

> Jesus answered, "Truly, truly, I say to you, unless one is born of water and the Spirit, he cannot enter the kingdom of God. That which is born of the flesh is flesh, and that which is born of the Spirit is spirit. Do not marvel that I said to you, 'You must be born again.' The wind blows where it wishes, and you hear its sound, but you do not know where it comes from or where it goes. So it is with everyone who is born of the Spirit" (John 3:5-8).

Ultimately what matters most is our relationship with Christ. The greatest consequence to our sin, to our deadly emotions, is enmity with God and a lack of peace in our lives. Our spirit man should be deeply grieved when we are in a place of bondage. God's heart grieves to see us there, especially when all the tools for freedom are in His Word and in His leading if we're ready for the amazing, abundant, whole, healed, and powerful life ahead.

When we think of overcoming deadly emotions in our life, we mistakenly think of how we can get rid of them. But like most things, if we become obsessed with not doing it, we will most likely be driven to it. Your victory won't just be in the removal of deadly emotions from your life, but how and what you pursue instead. The better, "overcoming" approach is to seek God in a deeper way as you pursue love instead of fear, faithfulness instead of jealousy, self-control instead of lust, patience instead of anger, peace instead of stress, gentleness instead of shame, and kindness instead of pride.

20 FREEDOM ACTIONS

1. *Remember that the truth will set us free.* Ask God to give you the wisdom and the discernment to recognize the lies in your life. Believe and stand on the truth in God's Word—the truth about who you are in Christ, the truth regarding your acceptance and your value, the truth in knowing you are to live in the eternal not in the temporal.

2. *The Christian journey is all about surrender.* We surrender when we accept Christ into our hearts as Savior, but we also surrender every day. Giving our jealousy, our fears, our inadequacies, our lust, our anger, our pride, our shame to Christ. This is an act of obedience that takes place every moment of our lives. When I get a feeling of jealousy, in that moment I have a choice to allow it to fester in my heart and poison my relationships or release it to God. My— our—security is in Him. The outcome of my—our—life is in His hands.

3. *Experience victory in the surrender.* First you must surrender your life to God's plan, but then there is another step…to savor and

acknowledge the victory in that act of surrender. If you struggle daily to give the control over to God, maybe you're not paying attention to the wonders that have taken place during those times you chose to or had to give a situation or a person over to God's best. These can be painful times, so we might focus on the pain more than the transformation that follows. And that transformation does follow. Share in the victory of the life you were meant to live!

4. *Embrace God's ways; release your own.* Many believers have been inspired by the story of missionary Jim Elliot and his four friends who moved to Ecuador to work with the Auca Indians. While their wives stayed at a base camp, the men set up a campsite close to the Aucas. Friends were worried about their safety while ministering in this dangerous area, but Jim knew it was God's calling. One of his famous journal entries provides his deep understanding of what it means to release one's life: "He is no fool who gives what he cannot keep, to gain what he cannot lose." Later these words would have great impact. Jim and his ministry partners were speared to death by the people they were committed to serving and leading to Christ.

The world looked at their deaths as a waste, but the men, women, and children who came to Christ because of their work, courage, and commitment would not agree. Jim Elliot was focused on the eternal, not the temporal. He believed in and lived out Paul's statement: "To live is Christ, and to die is gain" (Philippians 1:21). What about you? Are you willing to let go of the lifeless, temporal pursuits so that the eternal, godly pursuits are what you serve?

> *Nothings is really lost by a life of sacrifice, everything*
> *is lost by a failure to obey God's call.*
> Henry Parry Liddon

5. *Admit your shortcomings and your need.* When we keep things in the dark, in secret, the enemy has us right where he wants us. He

can use it against us every day and keep us in bondage. Once we have admitted or confessed our secret, God is able to deal with it and so are we.

During the time of my divorce it seemed as if the world was enticing me to medicate via its pleasure, as if the devil himself was injecting my thought life with poison. There were areas in my life I had not yet dealt with. There was shame I held on to, guilt I carried, and much unforgiveness resided in me. I experienced great pain from the divorce, but what held me in bondage and kept me from God's purpose in my life was the denial of these deadly emotions we've been discussing. Once I admitted they were in my life, I could tackle them with the tools we've explored together in this journey.

> *He cannot bless us unless he has us. When we try to keep within*
> *us an area that is our own, we try to keep an area of death.*
> *Therefore, in love, He claims all. There's no bargaining with Him.*
>
> C.S. LEWIS

6. *Recognize and turn from idols.* We have talked about tools that can effectively help us turn from our sin and the idols in our lives, the things that keep our hearts from being completely His. We need to let God cleanse away the dross in our lives so He can have a deep, intimate relationship with us. We can speak Christian lingo until we are blue in the face, but that doesn't bring connection to God. In our private world, the place no one sees but God, what are we saying to Him? Are we ready to repent and move away from our idols, big and small? Are we willing to recognize idols as anything we put ahead of God in our priority lineup?

7. *Accept who you are, where you're at, and where you're going.* Let go of the past so you can finally have a future! We have all made wrong choices, but we are forgiven if we have repented. God releases us from those choices, and we must release ourselves. He is loving

and faithful to us. To be loving and faithful to God, we must understand where we are sinning and where we are falling short of His will and hope for us so that we can, in turn, give those areas to Him. What aspect of your character or your past do you deny? If you feel stuck, examine what you've been ignoring and accept these areas so you can move forward.

8. *Nurture your relationships.* If the enemy can keep us isolated, deadly emotions can grab ahold of us and keep us from healthy interactions. The way we are able to see God work is in and through our relationships. They are the way we love and feel loved, the way we forgive and are forgiven. We build intimacy in relationships, and it draws us closer to the heart of God. Why? Because relationships challenge us to live out faith, and faith causes us to grow spiritually, which causes us to be emotionally healthy. We sometimes think if we remain isolated there is less chance to be hurt, that we are safe. If we never leave our homes, the only thing we are safe from is a car accident. Emotional safety only comes from resting in our faith in God and His peace.

9. *Practice the art of forgiveness.* Forgive those who have hurt you, wounded you, or wronged you. When your anger is justified and retaliation feels like the more natural response—this is when you most need to forgive. We can always rationalize and come up with reasons to hang on to our deadly emotions. But just like a cavity left unfilled will eventually destroy a tooth, the anger and bitterness left unfilled by the power of forgiveness will eventually destroy our hearts.

10. *Live a gracious, grace-giving life.* Grace goes beyond forgiveness when we understand God's mercy. Grace extends compassion and acceptance and doesn't wait for others or ourselves to first stumble before it emerges. When we choose to live in God's grace, we want to celebrate and promote it. Show grace through small gestures and

kindnesses. Fill your language with words of encouragement and appreciation. Notice the goodness in others even if you disagree with the person or you don't know him or her. Consider the story of forgiveness I shared in chapter 6 about the Amish community who lost their sweet, precious children. They went beyond forgiveness and entered the realm of grace. Let it inspire you to this level of God's love.

11. *Walk in the Spirit.* Paul presents the two approaches we can take when faced with life's choices and demands. The first approach is the way of the flesh; the second is the way of the Spirit. Paul's pointed question to the Galatians is relevant to us: "After beginning with the Spirit, are you now trying to attain your goal by human effort?" (Galatians 3:3 NIV).

The second way is to see it through Jesus. When we are saved by Jesus Christ, the deadly emotion we are enslaved to, the bondage we are controlled by, is no longer able to hold us captive. There is a supernatural Source empowering us in every area of our lives—from our purity, our holy devotion to Him, our ministry life, our relationships, our purpose and destiny, and our ability to have the faith to please God.

As we surrender to God's sovereign rule in our lives, He enables us to be what He has called us to be. Paul said God must increase and we must decrease. Charles Spurgeon said it is "all of God." Out of our brokenness we can move forward to the next freedom action.

12. *Show people Christ.* Ask yourself, "Do I want people to see me or see what Christ has done through me?" When we express to others our need for Christ to overcome our deadly emotions, we are giving Him the credit for our hopes and our futures. We show that we are dependent on the Lord. A broken person recognizes her inability to accomplish anything apart from the strength of Christ. She sees her sin and need for deliverance. God's glory is then revealed.

13. *Understand that you have an adversary.* The very thought of the devil can be scary and threatening. But to not believe in the devil is to not comprehend there is one who comes to accuse us, to shame us, to keep us in bondage, to distract us from the purposes of God.

> Submit yourselves therefore to God. Resist the devil, and he will flee from you (James 4:7).

14. *Don't give the wrong culprit credit.* The flipside of the devil issue also can cause believers problems. That is when we give the devil credit for our problems or the power to alter our lives rather than taking responsibility for our bad choices and sin. The devil has no power over followers of Christ. He can't overtake us or destroy us unless we allow him that power through the root of sin. Sin is what destroys us, not the devil. He is the prince of darkness, the prince of this world, and he tempts us through the desires of our flesh. To not take ownership for our sin, and say the devil is responsible for the sin itself is to avoid authentic spiritual growth and healing.

To act as if the devil is everywhere and behind every situation is also an error. The Lord allows trials and tribulation to befall us in order for the growth and building of our character. Sometimes our situation is flat-out our doing, the result of the seven deadly emotions being active in our lives. When we take responsibility for the places we give these deadly emotions in our lives, we then begin the journey to freedom. When we live in denial and blame the devil for our torment, we excuse ourselves from the responsibility, and we let go of the opportunity for freedom.

> *Never give in. Never give in. Never, never, never, never—in nothing, great or small, large or petty—never give in except to convictions of honor and good sense. Never yield to force; never yield to the apparently overwhelming might of the enemy.*
> Winston Churchill

15. *Rejoice and be glad.* I will never forget the day I accepted Christ and experienced complete forgiveness. I felt such excitement about this second chance. Reflect on when you felt the weight of the world lifted from your shoulders, from your spirit and were given the fullness of faith and love. Don't ever let that gladness and that celebration end. Instead, make each day a tribute to it.

The Israelites' deliverance from sorrow to gladness and from mourning to joy prompted them to have a feast to celebrate. They called this feast "The Feast of Purim," so the day of their deliverance would be remembered throughout every generation. They celebrate "The Feast of Purim" to this day. Mark your deliverance from the enemy's bondage in your life, for you have been given a new decree. God desires to prosper you, to deliver you and give you a hope for freedom (Jeremiah 29:11). Let it begin now.

16. *Have a heart for God.* During the rule of King Ahasuerus, Esther (a Jew), was made queen. She had a heart for God and for her people, and she knew her reign was due to the favor of God. She became aware her purpose as queen was more than serving in the royal court. She was to deliver her people from the hands of Haman, who devised a plan to destroy, kill, and annihilate all the Jews— young and old, women and children—in one day and plunder their goods (Esther 3:13). Esther trusted God to give her wisdom to walk out a plan to stop Haman, an enemy of the Jews. Esther's plan was accomplished, and the plan to annihilate the Jews disbanded. Imagine their joy, their relief, when they found out their kids would be okay, their families would be all right. Imagine their loyalty to the queen who delivered them from death.

Jesus died for us, to annihilate the plans of the enemy in our lives, to deliver us from bondage and set us free, to give us a plan and purpose for our lives—a plan for wholeness and hope for a future. He will restore to you what has been lost if you will turn to Him and seek Him and Him alone. Just as Haman had a plan for destruction in the lives of the Jews, so the enemy has a plan to destroy you. Esther was given wisdom in how to approach the king so he would stop this horrible plan from coming about. God will give you wisdom as you walk out His plan for freedom in your life. He will reveal to you the ways in which He desires to change you for His glory. This may feel uncomfortable at times, but we need to be comfortable with being uncomfortable. Change and transformation of hearts are never comfortable things.

> For I know the plans I have for you, declares the LORD, plans for wholeness and not for evil, to give you a future and a hope. Then you will call upon me and come and pray to me, and I will hear you. You will seek me and find me. When you seek me with all your heart, I will be found by you, declares the LORD, and I will restore your fortunes and gather you from all the nations and all the places where I have driven you, declares the LORD, and I will bring you back to the place from which I sent you into exile (Jeremiah 29:11-14).

17. *Get help for your journey.* If you need a counselor to help you overcome your deadly emotions, get a counselor; if you need a pastor or a safe friend, find one. Don't delay! When we try to do it alone, we take away the chance to feel God's strength through the support of others. And we keep ourselves stuck in the place of secrecy and aloneness. Speaking up about your need means that you'll have the opportunity later to speak up about God's goodness.

When I was going through my divorce and contemplating suicide, I had no one. I didn't want to be a burden to anyone so I didn't call or contact people close to me. I went through my torment alone, but I didn't have to. The first thing I did once I felt somewhat healthy again was pursue counseling with someone I could respect to mentor me. When left to our own devices the enemy is able to feed us lies. These lies appear as truth when we are in a place of desperation, so it is very important to find people who will speak truth to us when we are feeling like the lies are taking over. You have to find those godly people, whether they are in your church or they are counselors. This is not a time to be isolated. It feels overwhelming...the pain...but there is nothing you can't overcome with God on your side. He's with you, and He will strengthen you as you begin to walk out a new life in Him.

In the Bible there is a story of a lame man longing to be healed by Jesus. He is carried through a crowd by several friends. They fight their way through the masses and then actually lower him through the roof of a home because the crowd around Jesus is so big. The lame man could never have gotten to the feet of Jesus alone. He was too ill. When we are ill, it's hard for us to come to the foot of the cross alone. We need others to help us find our way. Reach out and get the help you need.

> Then they will seek My face; in their affliction they will earnestly seek Me (Hosea 5:15 NKJV).

18. *Have a fruit a day.* As we work through each deadly emotion by developing the fruit of the Spirit in our lives, we will harvest goodness and godliness. God is clear that we will know believers by their fruit. However, if we have the fruit in our lives but have no love, the rest is all in vain (1 Corinthians 13:1). Our effort and commitment should be a result of our relationship with Christ, not just the rules. Our fruit will come out of our love for Christ and nothing else.

> He who sows sparingly will also reap sparingly, and he who sows bountifully will also reap bountifully...He who supplies seed to the sower, and bread for food, supply and multiply the seed you have sown and increase the fruits of your righteousness (2 Corinthians 9:6-10 NKJV).

19. *Share your journey.* As your life is transformed by the process of eliminating the deadly emotions and their ties to your heart, you can share that amazing journey with others. The freedom actions that speak the most to you and your circumstances will also help lead you to a place of strength and authenticity. You'll share this

with others you meet and those you love by the way you treat them and the way you express God's heart to them.

Remarkable changes will take place as you release the emotions that bind you to the world and recapture the healthy emotions and instincts and leadings God has placed in you. Suddenly your life becomes limitless, and that's an incredible thing to share with everyone.

20. *Embrace a life of overcoming!* Getting free from deadly emotions is a wonderful, life-changing experience. When you walk out the purposes God has for your life in power and renewed strength, you will overcome your past, your obstacles, your insecurities, and your flaws by giving them all to God. The results are amazing when you stop trying to be the "fixer" of your own life and, instead, give your life over to the Perfecter of our Faith—Jesus. This journey isn't easy, but it is worth it! Relinquish the fear and rejoice in your freedom.

> Therefore, since we are surrounded by such a great cloud of witnesses, let us throw off everything that hinders and the sin that so easily entangles, and let us run with perseverance the race marked out for us. Let us fix our eyes on Jesus, the author and perfecter of our faith, who for the joy set before him endured the cross, scorning its shame, and sat down at the right hand of the throne of God. Consider him who endured such opposition from sinful men, so that you will not grow weary and lose heart (Hebrews 12:1-3 NIV).

Freedom Prayer for Ultimate Freedom

Lord, I long to come close to You. Revive my spirit, and set my crooked paths straight. I give up control in all these areas of my life—the fear, the jealousy, the lust, the anger, the shame, the stress, and the pride. I come to You and give You the control. I submit my will to You as an act of obedience. Lord, bring the wind, the power of the Holy Spirit, to fuel my life and to reveal the truth. Thank You, Jesus, for being everything to me. In Your name I pray. Amen.

> *The LORD will guide you continually,*
> *And satisfy your soul in drought,*
> *And strengthen your bones;*
> *You shall be like a watered garden,*
> *And like a spring of water, whose waters do not fail.*
>
> ISAIAH 58:11 NKJV

From My Heart to Yours

It is for freedom that Christ has set us free.
Stand firm, then, and do not let yourselves be
burdened again by a yoke of slavery.

GALATIANS 5:1 NIV

There's no condemnation in Christ Jesus! Be free and go into the world. Be salt and light (Matthew 5:13-14). Tell others of your freedom so the Lord will be glorified. My prayer for you, my friend, is that you will walk away from this journey with greater freedom in your life. We have a choice every day to choose Christ over our flesh, to sow the works of the Holy Spirit in our lives, and to reap a greater relationship with Christ. May the love of Christ be with you, and may He shine His face upon you.

Enjoy your freedom!

Michelle Borquez

Return Policy

<u>With a sales receipt</u>, a full refund in the original form of payment will be issued from any Barnes & Noble store for returns of new and unread books (except textbooks) and unopened music/DVDs/audio made within (i) 14 days of purchase from a Barnes & Noble retail store (except for purchases made by check less than 7 days prior to the date of return) or (ii) 14 days of delivery date for Barnes & Noble.com purchases (except for purchases made via PayPal). A store credit for the purchase price will be issued for (i) purchases made by check less than 7 days prior to the date of return, (ii) when a gift receipt is presented within 60 days of purchase, (iii) textbooks returned with a receipt within 14 days of purchase, or (iv) original purchase was made through Barnes & Noble.com via PayPal. Opened music/DVDs/audio may not be returned, but can be exchanged only for the same title if defective.

<u>After 14 days or without a sales receipt</u>, returns or exchanges will not be permitted.

Magazines, newspapers, and used books are not returnable. *Product not carried by Barnes & Noble or Barnes & Noble.com will not be accepted for return.*

Policy on receipt may appear in two sections.

Return Policy

<u>With a sales receipt</u>, a full refund in the original form of payment will be issued from any Barnes & Noble store for returns of new and unread books (except textbooks) and unopened music/DVDs/audio made within (i) 14 days of purchase from a Barnes & Noble retail store (except for purchases made by check less than 7 days prior to the date of return) or (ii) 14 days of delivery date for Barnes & Noble.com purchases (except for purchases made via PayPal). A store credit for the purchase price will be issued for (i) purchases made by check less than 7 days prior to the date of return, (ii) when a gift receipt is presented within 60 days of purchase, (iii) textbooks returned with a receipt within 14 days of purchase, or (iv) original purchase was made through Barnes & Noble.com via PayPal. Opened music/DVDs/audio may not be returned, but can be exchanged only for the same title if defective.

Bibliography

These resources were referenced while writing this book, and some are quoted within the book.

Cloud, Henry, and John Townsend. *Boundaries.* Grand Rapids, MI: Zondervan, 2002.

Crabb, Larry. *Shattered Dreams.* Colorado Springs: WaterBrook Press, 2002.

Dobson, James. *Bringing Up Boys.* Carol Stream, IL: Tyndale House Publishers, 2005.

Larimore, Walt, M.D., and Traci Mullins, contributor. *10 Essentials of Highly Healthy People.* Grand Rapids, MI: Zondervan, 2003.

Lewis, C.S. *Mere Christianity.* New York: HarperCollins, 1980, C.S. Lewis, Pte. Ltd.

Meyer, Joyce. *Managing Emotions.* New York: Warner Books Inc., 1997.

Roberts, Frances J. *Come Away My Beloved.* Uhrichsville, OH: Barbour Publishing, 2002.

Williams, Redford B., M.D., and Virginia Williams, Ph.D. *Anger Kills.* New York: HarperTorch, 1998.

❧ About the Author ❧

A woman of vision, Michelle Borquez's testimony is a powerful example of how God orchestrates our lives. Her blend of experience in ministry and business allows her to utilize every facet of her dynamic personality. In 1999 she founded *Shine Magazine,* and as editor-in-chief she conducted interviews with well-known personalities and ministry leaders, including Laura Bush, Anne Graham Lotz, Michael W. Smith, Kurt Warner, Chuck and Gena Norris, Beth Moore, and many more.

Currently the host of I-Life Television's *SHINE with Michelle Borquez,* Michelle is also the national spokesperson for Beth Moore's "Loving Well" television ministry special. As a gifted motivational speaker whose heart is for the wounded, Michelle focuses on helping people find restoration. She is founder and president of God Crazy Ministries, whose mission is to educate and edify the body of Christ and to share God's transforming power.

Michelle authored *God Crazy—An Adventurous Road Trip to Joyful Surrender* and coauthored *Live, Laugh, Love Again—A Christian Woman's Survival Guide for Divorce.* She's worked as a leading consultant for George Barna, John Maxwell's organization INJOY, Bee Alive, the American Association of Christian Counselors, Extraordinary Women, Family Restoration Ministries, and aided ministry leaders and church organizations in achieving their long-term goals.

The mother of four, Michelle and her family live in Tennessee.

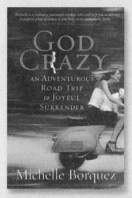

God Crazy
An Adventurous Road Trip to Joyful Surrender
Michelle Borquez

"God crazy" is the remarkable heart change that happens when you leap into God's purpose and never look back. After maintaining the appearance of an ideal marriage and life, Michelle Borquez's facade finally shattered. In that brokenness she discovered—as you can—a renewed, passionate love for Christ and a hunger for deeper faith. She leads you to that point of transformation where faith is not just a belief but your inspiration to soar as you...

- give your life over to God's lead
- embrace *la vida loca* ideas for your faith journey
- discover and pursue the desires of your heart

Other Great Harvest House Books

HOW TO FIND YOUR PERSONAL PATH TO SUCCESS
Keys to Living Out Your Purpose and Passion
Robin Chaddock

Do you sometimes question what you're doing? Do you wonder why you're here? Chaddock draws on her extensive experience as a life coach to help you find the God-given purpose that will bring you joy. She takes you step-by-step through a revealing process that uncovers your primary passions and greatest strengths, and then provides a framework for discovering how to use them to achieve satisfaction and fulfillment. Includes fun and challenging questions to help you identify core beliefs and clarify goals.

FROM FAKING IT TO FINDING GRACE
Discovering God Again When Your Faith Runs Dry
Connie Cavanaugh

Almost every believer experiences periods of dry faith or feeling disconnected from God. Sadly, nearly everyone stays quiet about their doubts, and they feel alone when they need support more than ever. Cavanaugh breaks the silence. Because she speaks out of her own 10-year struggle, you can trust her to understand and help you develop a deeper friendship with God. She says, "You may feel empty and alienated, but you're not alone!" She shows you how to look ahead as you focus on your God who loves you.

SEX, FOOD, AND GOD
Breaking Free from Temptations, Compulsions, and Addictions
David Eckman

Food, sex, and other great things created by God, can be misused to avoid emotional and relational pain. The resulting damage and desperation can be devastating. Offering compassionate understanding, Eckman shares how and why unhealthy appetites grip and trap people, how shame and guilt disappear when you realize God delights in you, and how four great experiences of the spiritual life break the addiction cycle. Grasp God's radical plan for freedom and escape aloneness and self-deception.

HOW TO SOLVE YOUR PEOPLE PROBLEMS
Dealing with Your Difficult Relationships
Alan Godwin

Make good relationships great and difficult relationships more positive! We all have people problems at times—disagreements, irritations, opinion differences, unreasonable requests. Drawing on years of counseling others and biblical wisdom, Godwin offers signs to look for and specific options for dealing with conflicts. Discover how to effectively handle conflict, avoid conflicts with unreasonable people, establish good communication, set healthy boundaries, and get back on track when old habits return.

HARVEST HOUSE
PUBLISHERS